THE FREE STATE

D. W. BROGAN

THE FREE STATE

SOME CONSIDERATIONS
ON ITS
PRACTICAL VALUE

"I question much whether we may not, by natural
means, account for the success of knaves, the calamities
of fools, with all the miseries in which men of sense
sometimes involve themselves, by quitting the direc-
tions of Prudence, and following the blind guidance
of a predominant passion; in short, for all the ordinary
phenomena which are imputed to Fortune; whom,
perhaps, men accuse with no less absurdity in life, than
a bad player complains of ill luck at the game of chess."

HENRY FIELDING—*Amelia*

HAMISH HAMILTON
LONDON

TO

DR. PIETER GERBRANDY

Prime Minister of the Netherlands

"Quod tanta animi fortitudine, sapientia, fide & constantia factum, ut quos populos huic vestro exemplo conferam, non inveniam. Atque hoc me inter alias causas movit, ut vobis hasce meas politicas meditationes inscriberem. Movit me etiam, quod in his saepissime pro illustrandis praeceptis politicis, exempla quoque a vobis, ab urbibus, constitutionibus, moribus, rebus gestis vestris & confoederatarum aliarum provinciarum Belgicarum desumpta petam."

JOHANNES ALTHUSIUS, *Ad Illustres Frisiae . . . Ordines*

First published 1945

PRINTED IN GREAT BRITAIN
BY WESTERN PRINTING SERVICES LTD., BRISTOL

CONTENTS

CHAPTER

PAGE

I. CASE FOR FREEDOM
7

II. CASE FOR POLITICS
46

III. LIBERTY AND ARMS
97

INTRODUCTION

THE character of this tract is explained, though its faults are not excused, by its origin as a tract directed to those intelligent Germans (who must exist) who may now be pondering the problem of why, twice in a generation, Germany has been involved in catastrophe—and has involved her neighbours. But it is possible that the sermon addressed to Germany may have a wider interest and application.

August 26th, 1944.

THE FREE STATE

CHAPTER ONE

CASE FOR FREEDOM

I

THERE is attributed to an American conservative, Fisher Ames, a famous contrast between democratic and non-democratic government. "Monarchy is like a splendid ship, with all sails set; it moves majestically on, then it hits a rock and sinks for ever. Democracy is like a raft. It never sinks but, damn it, your feet are always in the water."

Fisher Ames lived in the age of the American and French Revolutions; of one he approved a little, of the other he did not approve at all. But for all his dislike for the new forces loose in the world, for all his nostalgia for the past, he was too intelligent not to see the great new fact, that monarchy in the old sense had struck a rock and sunk for ever. He saw too the untidiness of democracy—and its permanence.

In the modern world, the historical background to the dictum of Fisher Ames has been forgotten. Men have forgotten the old world of the rule of custom, of the acceptance of the divine right, not only of kings but of republics. They have forgotten too the enthusiasm with which men welcomed the coming of the new age, the enthusiasm for a new world that greeted the news of the breaking of the cake of custom in France:

> "Bliss was it in that dawn to be alive,
> But to be young was very heaven."

So wrote Wordsworth. When the news of the Bastille came to the English Liberal Leader, Charles James Fox, he cried out, "How much the greatest event it is that ever happened in the world and how much the best." And in fairly remote Königsberg, Professor Kant for once was late; the great news from France was his excuse. Such enthusiasm could not last; the enthusiasm with which Fichte and Schiller received the news as well as the enthusiasm of Jefferson and Coleridge. Goethe could note, on the night of the battle of Valmy, that a new historical epoch had come into existence, but it was already a matter of war and *Hermann und Dorothea* told another side of the story of French and European liberation, illustrated the cost of the new birth. It is to Metternich (whose profession was to be reactionary) that there is usually attributed the joke: "when I saw what people did in the name of fraternity, I resolved if I had a brother to call him cousin." But warmer people than Metternich felt the same. Jefferson in America, Alfieri in Italy, Wordsworth in England, were all more or less disillusioned. The great voice of Burke was heard pleading with passion for the old, stable, moral order, only half silenced by the sight of the powers that had professed to fight for that sacred cause, taking time off to murder Poland.

From that disillusionment we have never totally recovered. But this did not matter so much as long as the memory of the old order was lively. The cruelty, war, extravagance of language, shallowness of thought, these did not matter so much as long as the hopes aroused by the Revolution, first in America, then in France, were continually fed by living memory of what the old order had been like. Men still knew enough to know that the old order had died; men still knew enough to know that it deserved to die; men still hoped enough to endure the birth pangs of the new world.

The old order was dead. The armies called into existence to resist the endless trouble-making of Napoleon marched, in form, to restore the old kings to their old places. But "there are no restorations." It was a generation, now, since a voice at Philadelphia, like gun shots at Concord, had been heard round the world: "We hold these truths to be self-evident, that all men are created equal, that they are endowed by their Creator with certain unalienable Rights, that among these are Life, Liberty, and the Pursuit of Happiness. That to secure these Rights, Governments are instituted among Men, deriving their just powers from the consent of the governed." Echoed in words in Paris, in arms from Madrid to Moscow, the principles of the Revolution set out on that long war that is still being fought.

Ever since that date men have sought to find other sources of political authority than "the consent of the governed," they have sought to achieve or have promised to achieve other aims of government than "Life, Liberty and the Pursuit of Happiness." But they have failed; they have been forced not so much to imitate democracy as to parody it, not so much to let men pursue happiness as to guarantee happiness, beating-up or killing the sceptics who have not been willing to admit that they were happy with the standard product issued from government store. The principle of traditional authority has been in retreat since 1776 and 1789; again and again substitutes for democracy have been announced, again and again new or old principles of political authority have been proclaimed. But as far as they were old and traditional, they have soon shown that all efficacy has been lost and as far as they have been new they have been bogus versions of democracy and not very new bogus versions at that, since the ancient world knew well what it meant by tyranny—and these new governments were tyrannies.

Yet in the past two generations there has been less fervour in the democratic faith, more scepticism about its performance and its premises. For one thing, the early democrats forgot, in their legitimate enthusiasm for their cause, that the power of any government or social arrangement to promote happiness is limited. As Jefferson wrote precisely, it is the *pursuit* of happiness that a democratic government exists to foster, to guarantee happiness, or even to promise it with a high degree of probability, is not the politics of a wise man. Shelley and the other anarchists could believe that only a few rotten institutions and corrupt men stood in the way of the liberation of the human race from its old bonds to slavery and death:

> "I met Murder on the way—
> He had a mask like Castlereagh."

But Castlereagh committed suicide and Kotzebue was assas-

A*

sinated without any notable improvement of the condition of the human race. Shelley had his doubts too:

> "Oh cease! must hate and death return?
> Cease! must men kill and die?
> Cease, drain not to its dregs the urn
> Of bitter prophecy.
> The world is weary of the past,
> Oh might it die or rest at last."

And Schiller, if he had lived longer, might have had doubts of the practical policy of the fraternity he sang in the Hymn to Joy. Some men felt that the error was in hoping much from government at all: before the great revolutionary question was asked, the great English Tory, Dr. Johnson, had given an answer:

> "How small, of all that human hearts endure,
> That part which laws or kings can cause or cure."

But this resignation was not easy or general; for if the power of kings and law, to cure the ills of human hearts was small, there was no doubt of their abundant and increasing ability to cause ills, old and new, to fall on the common man. And, faced with this fact, men became concerned to diminish evils done by law as well as to do good by law. That spirit, called by the English "utilitarian," saw in government an instrument of good or evil; it depended on how it was used. The Utilitarians neglected or, it would be safer to say, professed to neglect the emotional side of life, the passions for which men commit the unutilitarian mistake of dying, and this neglect in return produced an underestimate (especially in Germany) of the importance of the utilitarian attitude or of the degree to which it was compatible with the heroic, the unselfish, the romantic. In the western nations, especially, there was a kind of conspiracy to hide the warmth and passion of national life from the people. So we have, even at this moment, English soldiers in the sixth year of the war professing to be unable to say for what they are enduring death and wounds and exile and American aviators saying that they daily risk being burned alive to get a better ice-box. These soldiers are deceiving themselves or they are, very rightly, kidding the investigators. But it is more serious that they are deceiving the Germans, that they are preventing that people from realizing that it is again being beaten, not merely by superior military and economic resources but by a wiser, subtler, more deeply philosophical way of life.

There are many reasons why the early revolutionary hopes were deceived and why history, since 1776, has been one long struggle to get accepted as rules of practice what were then confidently asserted as self-evident truths. There are general philosophical criticisms that can be directed against the democratic theory so dogmatically stated by Jefferson; there is the inevitable disillusionment that comes when any governmental device is looked on as an end in itself and is then discovered to be an inadequate end. But there is also an important historical reason. In a very central and increasingly important part of Europe, the Revolution did not take. Germany was inoculated with the revolutionary germ by France, but the germ had a hard time of it, was never really at home and was exhausted by endless battles with the reactionary anti-bodies of the German body politic.

There are simple historical reasons why this happened. In the first place, the Revolution was suddenly imported into Germany before there was an effective demand for it. It came along with the French Army. There was no native German revolution; few native German revolutionaries. The Rights of Man entered Germany in the baggage wagons of a foreign army. It is not a good way to enter any country, though it may be the only way. Very soon the German was divided in his own mind between intelligent understanding of the fact that the French were sweeping away a great deal of totally useless lumber and resentment of the fact that it was *German* lumber being swept away by the *French*. Henceforward, the intelligent patriotic German was forced to say:

"Zwei Seelen wohnen, ach! in meiner Brust."

Down to the triumph of Bismarck it was doubtful which of the souls would win in the German breast; the soul that made the Germans part of the Western world or the soul which asserted that the Western world was wrong, that the Revolution and all it stood for, the Declaration of the Rights of Man, the Declaration of Independence, the Bill of Rights, all that we in the West mean by democratic ideals and democratic practice, was irrelevant, or unimportant, or wrong. The temptation to say the second was great because, otherwise, German political history was not as gratifying to German pride as every nation wants its history to be. If the West was right, Germany was not wrong but certainly belated. Nor was the motive necessarily ignoble. It is easy to think that Hegelianism is bad medicine for a society, especially for German society, without accusing Hegel of being servile or of being no wiser or profounder than the unfortunate Herr Fries whom he knocked about so roughly. It is also profitable to consider whether the rather foolish Herr Fries was not what the German people needed and to suspect that however valuable Hegelian profundity might have been in more pragmatic cultures in England, France and the United States, it was the last thing Germany needed if she was to grow up and get out of tutelage to princes and professors.

But Hegel and Bismarck had it, partly, again it should be admitted, by bad luck. If it had not been for the fantastically incompetent foreign policy of Napoleon III, Bismarck's great gamble might not have come off and the German people might not have been exposed to that most dreadful of temptations for a gambler, early winnings that tempt you to go on.

Historical speculation of this kind has only one value, to make mere moral or intellectual complacency harder and to remind us that nations, like men, can be unlucky. Germany has been unlucky—and that is something for which the whole world has to pay. But bad as it is to be unlucky, it is worse to be wrong about what constitutes your bad luck. For two generations the Germans have been moving to disasters involving them and their neighbours in greater and greater catastrophes; they have been conscious of some malign fate dogging their steps; they have given it a name from time to time: it has been the Jews or the English or the Russians or the Americans or the

French or all of them together. It is not; it has been the Germans; it has been the result, in the German community, of the failure of the German people to pass through a revolutionary epoch that, with more or less violence, threw it back to political first principles and forward to responsibility. The principles need not be very subtle; the first attempts at responsibility need not be very successful; but they must be the people's own political first principles and they must be the people's own mistakes.

The first stroke of bad luck for the Germans was that their sudden rise in economic and political importance, like their confrontation with the Revolution in arms, came before they had an adequate middle class to cope with the problems involved. Eighteenth-century Germany was poor and overwhelmingly rural. The middle class, such as it was, was economically and socially weak, timid, politically impotent. The equivalent of the numerous, rich, proud, aggressive, climbing bourgeois of England, France, Holland, did not exist. In one of the few real cities in Germany, one leavened by a large French bourgeois element, in Berlin, a third of the total population consisted of soldiers, officials and their families, all direct dependants of the King. Berlin was a larger Versailles or Windsor, not a bit like riotous, proud, gigantic, self-confident London; not a bit like huge, rebellious, militant, angry Paris. And most German cities were far smaller and far more prince-ridden than Berlin.

At no time in the nineteenth century were the new bourgeois classes in Germany in a moral or material position to free themselves from the ideas, the preferences, the prestige of the old military and civil bureaucracy. There were not, in nineteenth-century Germany, enough unofficial ideas or instruments of ideas to offset the immense power of the state machine, whether it was reflected in the army, in the bureaucracy, in the universities, state churches, state theatres. The idea of progress by free and wasteful competition, the Western willingness to trust to luck, had only a limited circulation in Germany. Germany was thus saved from many errors, from many types of bourgeois smugness, from many kinds of proletarian barbarism.

But she was also saved from life, from the chance of growing up.

Moreover, Germany was not only passing through the economic crisis, through the industrial revolution that was shaking all Western states; she was passing through a crisis of unification that other states, her neighbours, great and small, England and Holland, Switzerland and France, had long overcome. There was, in the double necessity, a temptation to get it over quickly, to build hastily with the existing materials. There was, in the success with which the building was done, or appeared to be done, a grave temptation to dizzy self-satisfaction. And since Germany was enriched and unified without undergoing the experiences of the Western lands, there was a temptation to ignore the lessons of Western history, to assert with pride that German experience was different and better. And since, again, the Western experience, its insistence on the intrinsic merits of the free political way of life, was an implicit criticism of the new German way, there was a temptation, to which many Germans succumbed, to retort that the German way was the true way, the richest and deepest type of political experience, a point of view which pleased the German state and, in Germany, points of view that pleased the state were the favoured points of view. Since past European history could not justify the German view, past European history was recast in German philosophical terms. A barrier was set up between Germany and the West; the true Germans thought the political experience of the West shallow, the West thought the German view of politics silly. Because of this barrier, Germany was less willing to understand either her own failures or her enemies' successes. She was the more willing to ignore the experience of others, in that her culture encouraged a vigorous handling of what less philosophical peoples call, the data of experience. Germany began to love the limitless and to despise peoples who had a preference for the defined.

"The notion that something that moves and lives, as genius does, can at the same time be absolute has some interesting implications. Such a genius and all its works must be unstable. As it has no external sources and no external objects, as its own past can exercise no control over it (for that would be the most lifeless of tyrannies), it is a sort of shooting star, with no guarantees for the future. This, for the complete egotist, has no terrors. A tragic end and a multitude of enemies may seem good to the absolute hero and necessary to his perfect heroism. In the same way, to be without a subject-matter or an audience may seem good to the absolute poet, who sings to himself as he goes, exclusively for the benefit of that glorious and fleeting moment. Genius could not be purer than that; although it might be hard to prove that it was a genius."[1]

It is not merely a question of bourgeois conformism in the West contrasted with heroic indifference to mere material pleasure or profit on the other side. The Germany of William II, like the Germany of Goering and Ley, was not a model of Spartan asceticism. And in the West, Spain had a greater contempt for mere comfort, mere wealth than had Germany— but with the other Western nations and, more perhaps than they, she preserved a profound sense of individual pride and dignity—a pride that (to the West) has always seemed inadequately developed in German culture, even before it was officially banned in the name of the *Führerprinzip*. To-day, it is harder and harder to see, in many cases, what the official German propagandists inside Germany mean; the language, not merely the Nazi jargon, but the ideas or passions expressed in the jargon, are strange to us. And behind that barrier of jargon and ideas, the German people, again defeated, more than ever distrusted and hated, has to undertake the terrible task of finding out what has again gone wrong, without the political tradition that might help her to state her problems. It is the claim of the Western culture that, in one great department of life, politics, the Germans are not profound pioneers or original barbarians, but backward members of the Western community who have gone more and more astray, through bad luck, through vanity, through neglect of the respect for the rights and spontaneous action of the individual for which German historical experience has so ill prepared the German people. That was their misfortune but is now their fault. They alone can cure the fault.

[1] Santayana, *Egotism in German Philosophy.*

Faced with the claims of general German culture, the Western world is willing to receive a great many of them. Madame de Staël, Matthew Arnold, Edgar Quinet, Renan, Green, Caird, Bosanquet, Burgess—the list of British, French, Americans who thought that they as individuals and their nations as societies had a great deal to learn from Germany could be lengthened indefinitely. The German spirit of *Geist* was what England needed, thought Matthew Arnold. The first enthusiastic labour of Edgar Quinet was a translation of Herder. To Göttingen went Americans like Motley, as long after went Frenchmen like Maritain to Heidelberg. There is no conspiracy against a German claim to be a great nation with a great culture, but there is, and has been, an increasing unwillingness to admit that German culture is to set, or has set, the pattern for Europe. On the contrary, German culture, like French culture, Spanish culture, English culture, is part of a total European culture, and if the Germans more and more refuse to accept the standards of that culture, there is not the slightest tendency to abandon the standards of the West, there is simply a new and critical examination of the aspects of German culture that lead to such an absurd result. There is no real movement to admire barbarism because it is vigorous or Germanic. The Gobineaus, Carlyles, Houston Stewart Chamberlains are eccentrics and some of the other, less interesting Western converts to German anti-European canons are mere pedants or worse.

And when faced with the formally legitimate developments of certain sides of German culture, the West refuses to follow. If they are legitimate children of Hegel or Wagner so much the worse for Hegel and Wagner. Above all, the extravagance of so much in German intellectual life, its delight in the un-limited, uncontrolled, undefined does not attract the West for long. This disciplined, ordered, planned wildness seems merely comic when it does not seem dangerous. Culturally, the West is willing to be tame if necessary; to be bound that it may be free: "Und das Gesetz nur kann uns Freiheit geben."

And so the contempt felt for bourgeois rationality, the moral superiority felt or expressed by many Germans at the sight of the pedestrian, utilitarian, prudent Western culture, evokes more amusement than anything else. That the whole civilized world has been wrong we do not believe, that heroism and extravagance are necessarily complementary ideas, this we do not believe. And the more Germans insist on it, the more they foster fear in our minds, fear that, in fact, modern Germanism and our ancient, growing and varied civilization are incompatible. Faced with this undefined German claim, in philosophy and in life, we are ill at ease. An English Hegelian, T. H. Green or Bernard Bosanquet, is embedded in a pragmatic society that saves him from the worst dangers of his trade; the habit of free discussion and of political responsibility saves an American political philosopher, like John Burgess of Columbia, from the worst dangers of his trade. Horace Williams of the University of North Carolina might keep Hegel's *Logic* in his desk drawer and study under Josiah Royce at Harvard, but William James was at Harvard, too, and Horace Williams had to live his life in the highly American world of North Carolina. It was good for him; it would have been good for Hegel.

For us, political philosophy has to be lived and cannot be lived vicariously. For us it is more important to let fools be foolish than, by putting down folly, to define wisdom too soon. The Athenians described the people who took no interest in politics as idiots. And we have no real admiration for the most efficient life of a nation of idiots.[1]

Of course many great men have neither taste nor talent for politics. They have better to do and as long as they act this way, because politics are *beneath* them, they are not mere idiots. It is to be feared that too many great Germans thought politics *above* them. And neither type of great man is the complete citizen or the complete great man. English and American and French institutions put only too many temptations, some might hold, in the way of writers, scientists, artists, thinking

[1] While an undergraduate at Oxford, I was once asked by a college servant if I was taking any interest in a current election. I replied, not quite truthfully, that I wasn't. "I believe, sir, that there were people in Ancient Greece called *idiotes*," was the merited rebuke.

themselves called on to advise or lead in politics. It is an extra-vagance, but a desirable extravagance, for these nations were enriched by waste as Germany was impoverished by thrift.

And this extravagance is a necessary element in the life of the free state. It is the aspect of democratic life—to which Fisher Ames drew attention when he said that "your feet are always in the water." But the wetness of the feet is a less serious evil than the dryness of the soul. William II was inordinately proud of the speed with which the streets of Berlin were cleaned after a storm, but other more important things were not done at all in his Berlin or Hitler's. When Paris or London was threatened with destruction and London was, in part, destroyed, the world felt that great centres of the human spirit were endangered; when Berlin was threatened it was realized how little in Berlin that was native to Berlin mattered to anybody who was not a German or, indeed, not a Berliner.[1] But there is more to be said than that. For the free society is not a mere raft; it, too, is a ship, a ship not like that which is wrecked on the reefs of human incalculability and unpredic-table destiny, but a ship like that which serves as the arms of Paris. And the motto of Paris is the motto of all free societies, "fluctuat nec mergitur." The ship of the free state may be wrecked but its cargo is never wholly lost—and, in fact, it does not often sink, not as often as the ship of the servile state, and that, when it does sink, takes with it all the cargo put in by timid voyagers.

[1] There is a story that William II asked Theodore Roosevelt why it was that so few American tourists came to his clean, efficient, modern Berlin, with its museums, carefully organized hygienic vice centres, concerts, etc., etc. "Go to Berlin, why, they would as soon think of going to Chicago or Glasgow."

II

No one knowing anything of life in America or in England or in France in the old free days would think of denying that there are serious drawbacks in the liberty of prophesying which is the essence of the free state. The lover of truth, the lover of his country, is often tempted to say with Jeremiah: "the prophets prophesy falsely, and the priests bear rule by their means; and my people love to have it so: and what will ye do in the end thereof?" The average man in the street in all countries may be a victim of his own ignorance, his own passion for rhetoric, his own defects in education, defects that may not be his fault but are, nevertheless, defects. There are moments when, let us say, the more vivid forms of religious and social eccentricity in Los Angeles, or even in London or Paris, seem to call out for an answer. And they get an answer, if you wait and do not fall back too hastily, in the manner of sixteenth-century Spain or twentieth-century Germany, on an imposed silence and an enforced orthodoxy. That temptation must be resisted. It must be resisted not only for the reason given, perhaps a little optimistically, by Milton, that truth will always win over error in a free and open encounter. It must be resisted not only for the more sceptical reason given by Justice Holmes, that many fighting creeds have been proved wrong and we are not, in fact, so certain of our premises as to be pragmatically safe in suppressing the conclusions of others, even the foolish, crackpot conclusions. We must resist the temptation for these reasons, and for the other reason that this suppression, this censorship, is so bad for the suppressors, the censors. It is very hard indeed to keep to the level of argument, or persuasion, when you have the level of force to tempt you. It was hard to argue with the Roman master of forty legions, no matter how sincerely a Hadrian or a Marcus Aurelius wanted you to argue with him, freely, sincerely, victoriously if need be. It was easier for the doctors of the Sorbonne to find monks than reasons, so their critic, Pascal, affirmed. It was easy to expel Jurieu and Bayle from France, to repeal the Edict of Nantes and then discover, too late, that the Church of Bossuet and Fénelon had left no heirs to answer Voltaire.

These three reasons are reasons enough why you must not only suffer fools gladly, as St. Paul says, but you must continue to suffer them even when they conspicuously stay fools. Suppression, the imposition of a uniform orthodoxy, whatever immediately gratifying results it may produce, gives, alas! no guarantee that the monopoly thus secured to one opinion will be secured to wisdom. Modern Germany has proof enough of that.

But there is another democratic reason why you must suffer fools gladly. The wind bloweth where it listeth. Out of the mouths of babes and sucklings has come wisdom in the past. It was the child in Hans Andersen's story who alone saw, or alone said, that the Emperor had no clothes. The plain man, the stupid man, has often this gift of unsophisticated sight; a courtier never has it (and a Grand Inquisitor has his court too). Nor is the sufficient wisdom of one age and one class likely to be adequate to the needs of other ages and other classes. The Inquisitor may forget the sacred truth he is charged to protect; he may, like Dostoievsky's Inquisitor, strongly dislike it. He may, like the Templars, fight in public for a faith he derides in private. He may be like the Indian King in Mr. H. G. Wells's fable, who in building a vast tomb for his wife, forgot her, and forget why it is that he is vigilantly on guard outside the Holy Office or the Gestapo prison. All he will remember of his duties is the duty of death and the pleasure of torture.

Then there are so few really original human spirits; the human race is not rich enough in genius to be able to afford to allow the decision who is to be fostered, who is to be neglected or killed, to be purely a state matter. It is not only a matter of a career open to orthodox talents; that is important, but it is a thing that a tyranny can manage as well as mediocre democracies, though not as well as good democracies. But the social organization must be such that it not merely gives a chance to Euler or Laplace but does not, by stupidity, distort the genius of a Ramanujan. It must allow for the risks of not finding Giottos on the hills as well as for the social risks of excluding Hitlers from an art school. It must diminish as much as possible the risk of embittering the lives of mediocre people, or even incompetent people, by making them feel that, even if they were as good as at moments they think they are, they would still have no chance of acceptation. No democratic society perfectly provides for this problem. The United States does it better than England; in some ways England did it better than France.

But any organization of science, the arts, the theatre that decides *a priori* what are the permissible doctrines, what the classes or races or groups in which alone genius will be recognized, by that alone decides that the national life will be poorer than it need have been. In nothing is the Führer principle more deadly than in the life of the spirit. *Geist* cannot be *gleichgeschaltet*. Napoleon, noting that there was no literature in France and writing, "let the Minister of the Interior see to it," has long been a joke. But, as Albert Thibaudet says, if all the good writers of France were in exile under Napoleon, there was one exception, the Emperor himself. No such comfort can be taken by the subjects of the author of *Mein Kampf*. To decide that the only real function of the scholar, the artist, the scientist, is to support the claims and accept the priorities laid down for him by politicians, even if those politicians are tyrants as well, is to take great liberties with the unpredictable life of the human spirit. There is not so much of it that we can afford to plan it:

> "For sparing of his sacred strength, not often,
> Among us darkling here, the Lord of Light
> Makes manifest his music and his might."

Can we believe for a moment that the dying or the living Goethe would have allowed his ration of light to be allotted to him by the Grand Duke? Patrons can get great music and great architecture with some ease, since the musician and the architect want, above all, material facilities which the patron commands, without which the composer and the architect may be helpless, with cathedrals and symphonies existing only on paper. But for the writer it is harder, much harder, to let the patron choose what to patronize. The temptation is more subtle; it is harder to give an ideological content to a sonata or to an opera or a chancellery than it is to impress on even a lyrical poem, or a novel, views of life, of destiny, of morals that may or may not meet the approval of the rulers. The Roman poets of the Republic were not better poets than the great court poets of Augustus, but even Virgil and Horace made concessions of dignity and manly decorum unthinkable to Lucretius or Catullus. Milton did better neglected by Charles II than employed by Cromwell; Dante wrote his poem in exile; Wagner was none the worse for having been a rebel and none the better for having to be a courtier. To try to confine the human spirit to good party men, to exclude Jews, Negroes, Indians, Poles, from the possibility of developing their gifts, to exclude unorthodox Germans from the possibility, this is to take a very grave responsibility before history, the responsibility taken by those who reduced Spain to an orthodox sterility in which no Vittoria, no St. Teresa, no Cervantes or Calderon broke the orthodox silence from which more than heresy had been extirpated.

The German tradition of freedom on this point was not strongly established even before Hitler reduced to obscene parody all the arguments for directing culture in the way it should go. This cultural freedom has lacked institutional backing and heroic figures. It is possible to argue successfully that Hegel was not a servile Prussian-bought lickspittle, but it is significant that it has to be argued. An English poet, Browning, wrote one of his most famous poems on the theme of the traitor poet:

> "Just for a handful of silver he left us,
> Just for a riband to stick in his coat."

Too many German intellectuals seem to the outside world to desert their own people, the people of the spirit and the German people alike, less for the handful of silver (which the people can give you in other ways) than for the riband to stick in the coat, which only the Prince or the Führer can give. Browning in his protest was able to call on Milton, Burns, Shelley, even on Shakespeare (who had a healthy eye for the handful of silver). It would be harder for a German poet. Harder, but not too hard, to-day. For he has only to ask himself how in Hitler's Germany you can produce *Don Carlos* and leave the Marquis Posa as Schiller left him, an insult to the Führer, or how to produce *Fidelio* without making it an attack on Himmler, how to produce the *Meistersinger* without making fun of the Reich Chamber of Culture, how to deal with the pre-eminent place of Luther's Bible in the history of German prose without being forced to contrast its Jewish contents with the contents of the Nazi prophetical books and the style of Luther, nourished on Jewish wisdom, with the style of the purifier of the German race.

And this is the solution of a problem on which clever Germans have wasted much thought and wind. How is it that so commercially minded a people as the Americans (look at what they say of themselves in *Babbitt*) produce Emerson and Thoreau and Robert E. Lee and William James, practitioners and practisers of the free and heroic life? Look at the French— see what Molière and Flaubert and Bernanos, their countrymen, say, yet they produce Joan of Arc and the army of Verdun and the army of the Interior, that great, free army of Liberation which makes the German legend of 1813 seem thin and poor! Look at the English, that smug, greedy, uncritical people of poets, philosophers, romantic heroes like Nelson, sagacious heroes like Wellington, that nation of shopkeepers and home of the R.A.F. How can the smug, utilitarian Swiss still be the countrymen of Winkelried and Tell? It is simply by *practising* the political virtues of liberty and wisdom instead of making theories a substitute for practice and responsibility. And in the Western world the compatibility of a good life for the grocer and the possibility of heroism for the hero (who may turn out to be a grocer too) has been taken so much for granted that certain German criticisms have got less attention than they deserved. They seemed merely silly, and so negligible. They are not negligible.

Again and again in modern times the Western world has been faced with a parade of hostility to its fundamental principles which it has found it hard to take seriously. That very talented or, at any rate, young talented men should talk and write of violent, complete solutions, solutions to problems that they state violently and fantastically, is all in the day's work. That the state and nation should be turned upside down, the "great work of time," the national life, made by wise and prudent as well as by rash and original men, brought to ruin to suit the emotional and aesthetic needs of young men in search of a philosophy, seemed to us foolishness, not to be taken seriously. We were very startled when we found Germans taking it seriously.

Nothing, in a sense, was more natural than this mutual incomprehension. The long, painful, chastening political education of the West had taught the Western peoples that the national life was no matter for artistic experiment. Politics was itself a great and subtle art with its own rules and inner life and no more to be recast in merely literary terms than painting is to be recast in purely musical terms. The fatal separation of the German intellectual classes and artistic classes from the common and often drab responsibilities of citizenship, was here paid for in the production of a class of politically blind persons of talent. Thus one of the prophets of the Third Reich, indeed the inventor of the name, Moeller van den Bruck, was too intelligent not to see that the political life of France and England was far more closely united to the national culture than was the case in Germany; the English and the French peoples were far more soaked in their national tradition than were the German masses. There was nothing surprising in this; there had been no German national political life for anybody to be soaked in, no time for national habits to become second nature for the Germans. This was hard on the Germans, no doubt. But the realization of this fact was too hard for Moeller van den Bruck. For in the close interweaving of the nation and the state, the national culture and the political institutions of France and Britain, he saw mediocrity, hypocrisy, utilitarianism. The German was not belated, he was a pioneer; he was right to despise these characterless societies, these systemless systems of the West. In face of the fact that these societies *did* do what the Prussian state had failed to do, he refused to see that the integration of the national life was the result of the free institutions of these countries, of that long political education in the *tacte des choses possibles*, in that reconciliation of the hard facts of this terrestrial life with the aspirations of mankind. One lesson of that education was that states do not exist for the gratification of the aesthetic sensibilities of people like Moeller van den Bruck or Ludwig II or William Beckford or any other extravagant figures, however talented, however valuable in other ways. Another lesson was that the free societies do, in fact, allow for the production in adequate numbers of this type, and do in fact produce, in addition, as many pure artists of the highest type as do societies of the type dreamed of by Moeller van den Bruck. They produce a great many people of all kinds because they let them produce themselves.

In the Englishmen, Americans, Frenchmen, Dutchmen who angered Germans of this type, there were no doubt many Philistines (if we may borrow a German word for a type that if not exclusively German, is yet German enough). There were plenty of men in authority in these countries who were contemptuous of the spirit, to whom *Geist* meant nothing. But they were not in exclusive control; nobody was in exclusive control. That was the system.

But to intelligent Frenchmen or Englishmen or Americans, none of whom were in the least likely to be uncritical admirers of their own country, the ideas of Germans of this school seemed to be substitutes for reality. The German language lent itself to a nominalist view of life; words could easily be mistaken for reality. Thus thoughts about culture could be a substitute for the contents and life of a culture. It was not true that German culture was richer, more inspiring, more worth imitating than French or English culture. Nobody in fact believed this, not even the Germans, least of all the great Germans. In the same way the history of the West was not less romantic, daring, original, than that of Germany. The great sea nations, England, Norway, Holland, might have laughed at being asked to think themselves as prosaic, timid, huggers of safety, avoiders of adventure. Even in the twentieth century the sea does not allow people like that to make money out of her—and these peoples did make money out of the sea on the sea's highly exacting terms.

The Americans, with their three-hundred-year-old Western advance across the continent, had not had wealth handed to them on a platter and were not likely to be struck dumb with regret and admiration for the thwarted Eastern advance of the twelfth-century Germans or to be induced to speculation about what might have happened if Henry the Lion, not Frederick Barbarossa, had triumphed. The world could not reasonably be expected to spend so much time as that over German spilled milk and could not be prevented from thinking that such lamenting over the past, like such fact-despising theories in the present, were proofs that Germany was indeed a young nation, young, not in virility, but in the emotional instability and easy self-pity of adolescence. The sorrows of young Germany seemed only too like the sorrows of young Werther and it was time that Germany outgrew them.

This was concealed from the Germans by two admirable aspects of Western life; its passion for general justice and its devotion to self-criticism. Justice for Germany was an ideal common to the Germans and to the increasingly numerous critics of Versailles. But for the Western critics, justice for Germany was a good thing because it was justice; for the German revisionists it was a good thing because it was justice for Germany. They had no very visible interest in justice for other people. What Germans rejoiced that the Treaty had at least ended a shabby and almost pointless breach of faith with Denmark, that what the Germans had not wished or had not been able to do had been done for them, that in North Schleswig the promise of a plebiscite made by Bismarck in 1864 had been carried out by the Allies in 1919? What Germans sought means of making reparation, moral as well as material, to Belgium, what act of national repentance was suggested?

It was one of the greatest grievances of the Nazi philosophers that the virile, quick-breeding German people should be crowded in on less territory (after Versailles) than the dwindling French. In insisting on a high birth-rate as a proof of national energy, the Nazis were not wrong as compared with the complacent Malthusians of the West, but German fecundity was very far from being a problem, or that kind of problem, and if fecundity were the sign of national greatness and national energy, the nations with a future were the Slavs, the hated Russians, and the despised Poles. Compared with them the population differences between the Germans, the English and the French were trifling and compared with the strain on the peasants round Cracow, the strain on the inhabitants of the Ruhr was slight. As long as Germany was manœuvring for concessions, as long as Stresemann, the politician who deserved best of the German nation (whatever view Europe may take of his career), was still limited to "finessing," the real gulf between the Western friends of Germany and the German friends of Germany was hidden. Stresemann was seen as a kind of Mazzini or Gladstone because he could not demand, he could only negotiate.

But when the Germans ceased to be limited by the conditions imposed in 1919, the cleavage was made evident. If the Germans had been badly treated in the Ruhr by the French, how were the Jews now treated in the Reich? Then it was discovered that the difference was that the Jews were not Germans, in a deep sense a German *could not* be unjust to a Jew no matter what he did. It took the Western nations some time to learn this lesson; there had been a deep emotional and personal investment in the view that the difference in verbal formulas between so many Germans and the mass of Westerners were verbal only. But it was not verbal only; there was in Germany an old, sophisticated, ingenious and sometimes subtle reaction against the Rights of Man, that foreign, Anglo-American-French importation. On that foundation, built by poets, orators, artists and some people whom it is not mere convention to call thinkers, a new system of non-political government, an artificially barbarous tyranny was built. And the West, faced with this monstrous growth, began to come out of its dream of a political religion of all sensible men. The wars of religion were back. Adam Wayne, the Provost of Notting Hill in Chesterton's prophetic fable, had been right. "When I was young I remember, in the old dreary days, wiseacres used to write books about how trains would go faster, and all the world would be one empire, and tram-cars go to the moon. And even as a child I used to say to myself, 'Far more likely that we shall go on the crusades again, or worship the gods of the city.'"

And it is essential for the Germans to realize (it must be repeated) that Adam Wayne is right. There is no hope of converting the West to the German view of the world; what are its most German aspects seem to the West to be mere compensations for the sadder sides of German history. But that there has been no equivalent in Germany of the political life of the West is not a reason for our consenting to undervalue our inheritance. It is not for us to invent theories to explain away the limitations of German historical experience; we have enough to do with the real defects of our own. But the insistence on freedom, the scepticism of mere authority, of mere efficiency, the belief that no convenient fiction of corporate life should be allowed to hide the ineluctable fact of individual existence, that we are often united but never fused; these will remain.

And any society that submerges the citizen in the obedient subject, that induces the subject to divinize the ruler, that makes the idol of Divus Cæsar, or the Divine Kings of the East, the symbol of Society, will seem unworthy of our traditions, as it was unworthy of the traditions of Greece faced with Persia, of the Hellenic world faced with the claims of Alexander, of the Roman state corrupted by power, sinking from a republic to an empire. Unless the German people realize the degree to which the whole ethos of Nazi-ism was incapable of winning support in the West, except from the base and timid, while in Germany, alas! it won support from the brave and energetic as well, the nature of the barrier between them and the Western victors will be misunderstood.

It is naturally difficult for people brought up in a formal, directed culture to recognize not merely the value but the existence of the spontaneous authority of the free society. Thus even a very intelligent German, knowing both the language and the culture of a free state but without any real assimilation of its spirit, can make the most astonishing and, from the point of view of the German nation, disastrous mistakes. It is not merely that Germany has had to pay for the follies of intelligent maniacs like Holstein or of frivolous fools like Ribbentrop, but even intelligent and sensible Germans have helped to erect a barrier of misapprehension that has led to an underestimate both of English and American character and power.

Thus William Dibelius told his countrymen after their defeat in 1918 a great many things that it was desirable that they should know, but he also told them a great many things about the English that were untrue and dangerously untrue, simply because he was unable to move outside the German categories of law and authority and because, for obvious reasons, he had not seen the English state drawing on the immense reserves of force and authority on which the free state *can* draw in a great crisis, because it has not prevented their accumulation in ordinary times. So Dibelius described the people who were, alone, in the summer of 1940, to resist the Third Reich in the moment of its triumph—and resist without panic, without terror, and with very little call on the coercive power of the state—as unable to understand that "a social life comprising millions has got to have its details organized." For mere social integration and acceptance of detailed control as necessary, England in the great crisis was a model. An English queue forming under bomb threats, breaking up under imminent danger and reforming immediately the danger is past, is an interesting confutation of the interesting theory of Professor Dibelius and has been an interesting example of the obstacles that the habits of freedom have put in the way of the agents of the habit of obedience.

Of course, in a society in which no official has uncontrolled authority and there is no hereditary reverence for official wisdom and only a fairly recent habit of spontaneous obedience to the extension of the authority of the state, there will be many ragged edges, distressing to German minds in which material tidiness has always been the compensating force to offset theoretical extravagance. You can allow your subjects unlimited freedom of dangerous thought if you allow no freedom of inconvenient action. Then, apart from individual untidiness, there is institutional untidiness. If you allow independent corporations real freedom of action you cannot guarantee that their policy will run in harness with yours. Thus, when the British Government of the day was determinedly refusing to note the real character of the Third Reich and some British political and diplomatic officials were taking a "boys will be boys" line, not noticing that Goering and even Baldur von Schirach were hardly boys and forgetting how nasty bad boys can be, the British universities refused to play. Ambassadors could go to the *Parteitag* but the universities refused to join with their German colleagues in celebrating the great festival of the enslavement of the ancient and once dignified University of Heidelberg. And, the third centenary of Harvard University occurring at about the same time, the British universities were able to show their lack of the German version of the team spirit by celebrating that anniversary with almost offensive enthusiasm—offensive to the German universities, that is.

Even institutions, traditionally spokesmen for state authority and bulwarks of the established order, are unmanageable in free societies, especially in free societies which have encouraged or tolerated free institutions inside the state. In modern times, at least, the state Church in England has been far from being a docile agent of the state. At the time when uncritical British imperialism was at its height and national complacency at its most offensive, in the very capital city of the imperialist movement, Birmingham, the Anglican bishop, Charles Gore, was a determined opponent of the whole policy associated with the name of Birmingham's chief citizen, Joseph Chamberlain. When the Putumayo rubber atrocities were being exposed by a great British public servant, Roger Casement (later hanged as a traitor—i.e., Irish patriot—by the British Government in 1916), the British shareholders who gained by this exploitation were denounced in person by Dr. Hensley Henson in West-minster Abbey in London. (Dr. Henson was later made Bishop of Durham, one of the four great offices of the Church of England.) When the English name was being disgraced in Ireland by the "Black and Tans," one of the decisive steps taken to end this comparatively mild forerunner of the S.S. was a speech in the House of Lords by the Archbishop of Canterbury who, on retirement, was made Lord Davidson. These are only a few British instances of those failures in the team spirit that are necessarily characteristic of free societies.[1]

[1] These failures may have no relevance to the value of the dissent from official policy. They may arise from the fact that X having a right to do his duty as he sees it and Y having a right to do his duty as *he* sees it, and neither X or Y being on good or any terms, they do different things. And the outside spectator, not used to the mechanical defects of free societies, may see deep cunning and Machiavellian duplicity in what is mere incoherence. On July 21st, 1911, at the height of the Agadir crisis, when the second Reich had sought to intimidate Britain and France by sending a gunboat (*Panther*, the Germans run to form in nomenclature) to Agadir, "bankers were dining at the Mansion House. Two things happened at that dinner which, if England had been a continental nation, everyone would have assumed to have been concerted. Perhaps continentals did assume this; but there is not the least reason to suppose that if they did they were right. The peace-loving Chancellor of the Exchequer (Mr. Lloyd George) hoisted a danger signal, in his 'Agadir' speech; there were some things in the international sphere that England would not stand. Many people overlooked the signal. But as it was made in the general code of diplomacy, diplomats everywhere read it with ease. After him, the Governor of the Bank, A. C. Cole, rose to explain that his Court (i.e. the Directors of the Bank) had agreed—at last, though this he did not say—to fall in with the suggestion which had long been before the City that the Directors of the Bank and representatives of the clearing bankers should hold regular quarterly meetings, to discuss matters of common interest. He spoke of no international complications. Probably he did not think of any. Certainly the Bank's decision to act had nothing to do with the Chancellor's decision to speak; the Bank and that Chancellor

Suspicion of the spontaneity of the movement of public opinion, the conviction that any important action *must* have been planned, these are natural results of training in a society like the German, in which it is possible to hold, sincerely, the idea that the English are not really a law-respecting people! The degree to which the political or economic rulers are in command of the situation is overestimated, the degree to which they are part of a total environment to which the feeling of obscure people and the moral and intellectual choices of the anonymous masses contribute a great deal and often set the limits of the possible, is underestimated. And they are especially ignored when the British or American state acts successfully under apparent moral pressure from its own people and in the name of moral principles which it may have only slowly and reluctantly accepted as relevant. To men of the Frederickian or Bismarckian tradition, such professions of moral principles must seem hypocritical and success in a policy based on them *must* be the result of careful planning.

The success with which the English, the Americans, the free peoples, have more than once mobilized world opinion against Germany has naturally attracted the attention and caused the resentment of patriotic Germans of all kinds. Even the most credulous German, forced to look at the kind of sympathizer *he* can induce to see the brighter side of German policy and German methods, is assailed, if not with doubts, at any rate with envy. Sven Hedin with his doubtful pedigree, George Sylvester Viereck, with his limited success, Joyce and Kaltenbach, Déat and Laval, Mussert and Quisling, are these the best that can be won to see the need for the saving the world by Germanic methods? Noticing that the English and Americans get their claims to moral principle, their assertion that there is a general, not merely national, interest in *their* victory, much

were not intimate in any case." (Clapham, *The Bank of England*, Volume II, pp. 413–4.) There is no doubt that continentals (and not only German continentals) will find this hard to believe. They may even refuse to believe it, preferring to assume that either Sir John Clapham is deceiving them, or that he is a simple man whom the Bank of England has found it easy to deceive. In either case, they would be wrong.

more easily accepted than any German pretensions are, the German seeks an explanation that will not force him to think out again the bases of German thought and action, to consider afresh what may be wrong with German political habits.

One German answer, made in good faith by intelligent Germans, is that the moral language and moral force available in England are used by the English Government as part of its political equipment, like the Navy or the Bank of England. Even if this were so, it would be worth investigating more objectively why England (and the United States) are so rich in political assets of this kind. You may represent the agitation over the atrocities associated with the rubber business in the Congo Free State as being turned on and off as it suited the British Government. "Even the Government was ready to lend an ear; it wanted to attach Belgium to the anti-German Entente; here was a means of exerting pressure upon it. Once that end was attained, official England found, all at once, that the reports from Africa were grossly exaggerated. Morel continued his agitation unweariedly, but the response from public opinion and the Government obviously grew fainter, and the fearless idealist began to speak with unconcealed bitterness of the duplicity of his own Government."[1] Taking a leaf out of Chesterton's book, I shall improve on Professor Dibelius's Machiavellian explanation of this moral profiteering. The British Government, when it launched this attack, knew that the Congo Free State, run by Leopold II of Belgium as his private property, was destined sooner or later to pass into the control of the Belgian Government (which *pace* Dibelius did not control the Free State when the agitation began). It knew too that the Belgian Parliamentarians would survive while the old and sinful King was sure to die soon. By making it easy to bring pressure to bear on the King, it got the Belgian Parliamentarians into its debt and was so able to involve them in that conspiracy against Germany for which Belgium has been twice rightly rewarded by preventive invasion by the Reich. How's that, umpire?

But the Dibelius theory will not, in fact, stand much

[1] Dibelius, *England* (English translation), pp. 106–7.

B

examination, though at its own level of naïve sophistication it will stand a great deal of extension. If the Armenian agitation of 1896 fizzled out, the reasons, as any student of the policies of the Germany of William II knows, were not exclusively English. A little reflection would have shown the difficulties of an explanation which covers Gladstone's successful campaign of 1878 against the Bulgarian atrocities committed by Turkey (the traditional ally of Britain, the prop of British foreign policy), and his corresponding unsuccessful campaign of 1896 against the atrocities committed against Armenians by the traditional ally, success or failure being seen simply in terms of the policy of the Government. For at the head of the Government in 1896 was Lord Salisbury, who had been one of the most important members of the Government in 1878. He, it can be said, was consistent. But what Dibelius fails to explain is why, in 1880, Gladstone became head of the Government, defeating Disraeli and Salisbury alike? That, in a free state, there is no really effective means of turning on and off the moral indignation of the country may be hard to believe, but it is true. If you can turn it off, it is not there in adequate quantities in the first place.

Of course, the moral sense of the British or the American public is often torpid, is often stupid, is often ill-informed, is often put into cold storage under the pressure of patriotic emotion, is less often but sometimes ignominiously diverted from its object by gross material greed. It was in full consciousness of this saddening truth that Chesterton wrote to an ally in the opposition to the Boer War. "There are two cries always capable of raising the English in their madness—one that the Union Jack is being pulled down, and one that the Pope is being set up. And upon the man who raises one of them responsibility will lie heavy till the Last Day. For when they are raised, the best are mixed with the worst, every rational compromise is dashed to pieces, every opponent is given credit for the worst that the worst of his allies has by his worst enemy been said to have said. 'That horror of darkness swept across us when the war began.' . . ."[1]

[1] Ward, *Gilbert Keith Chesterton*, p. 250.

What could a German say more, what could any German say as well? But it was because Chesterton had said that; because he had opposed what he thought an unjust war, that his support of what he thought a just war had influence inside and outside England. It was for this reason that his tract, *The Crimes of England*, had such effect. For it was in great part an admission of many crimes in England and notably what he thought the crime of supporting the barbaric state of Prussia in the eighteenth century. It dwelt, too, on other crimes and provided the German controversialist with plenty of ammunition which, however, could hardly have been heard over the great gun of Chesterton's affirmation that the war of 1914 was *not a crime of England but a reparation of crime*.[1] It was because the English tradition gave plenty of room for political dissent that the assent of men like Chesterton, Wells and others was important. It was because that assent was not given unconditionally, automatically, that it was worth having. Both Chesterton and Mr. Wells for different reasons, later thought they had been imposed on in detail and said so at length; they did not think they had been imposed on in gross, that Germany had been right. The disillusioned Morel had further reason to be disillusioned in the war, for he was a victim, by the nursery standards of that day, to the mild intolerance of that day. So was Bertrand Russell. All the more reason then to note that Bertrand Russell supports this war.

In the controversial battles fought between nations victory goes, in fact, to the nations for which the battles are not mere tactics, the nations in which the conflicts over international justice inside a nation are not mere sham fights.

The same point is illustrated abundantly by American history. That history is not a uniform story of righteousness, but then Americans have never pretended that it was. The writing of a "Crimes of America" would be a shorter job than a

---

[1] As a schoolboy in Scotland during the last war, I was given *The Crimes of England* (with half a dozen other books, mainly poetry) when ill with mumps, to aid my recovery. William McIntyre, then and now, was not indulging in any deep double bluff in political morals. He was a Scottish not a Prussian teacher.

"Crimes of England," because the United States is a younger nation. But great Americans have contributed and will contribute generously to the criticism of the sins and mistakes of the American Government and people. American schoolboys and girls learn to admire and even to read some of the poems of James Russell Lowell, but Lowell's most original work was done as a satirist of the politicians, the soldiers, the people of his own country. *The Biglow Papers* is a bitter attack on a glorious and successful but, Lowell thought, wicked American war, the Mexican War. And whether that war was as wicked as Lowell thought is still a matter of controversy in America—and that it is a matter of controversy has been an important political fact. It made it far harder for those Americans who, for whatever reasons, wished to exercise the overwhelming power of the United States against Mexico in the revolutionary years of this century, to have their way. Mexico has been allowed to find her own equilibrium, which is not a "Yankee" equilibrium, at considerable American cost in money and what old-fashioned diplomatists call prestige and old-fashioned soldiers, honour. And Mexico which, in 1917, the Second Reich hoped, not quite foolishly, to involve in war against the United States, was the first of the great Latin-American states to support the policy of the United States in organizing resistance to the Third Reich in the Americas.

This summer (1944), there died in exile in America, on the eve of triumph, Manuel Quezon, President-in-exile of the Philippine Commonwealth. He had begun political life fighting against the Americans, he had come to the front under American rule as head of the party determined to end that rule. And he died, confident in the promise of the American government and the American people that they would both drive out the Japanese and free the Filipinos. He had reason for the confidence, in part because there had been in 1898 so many distinguished Americans and so many plain Americans who thought he was right. Great men of letters like Mark Twain, great business magnates like Andrew Carnegie, great political leaders like Senator Hoar and Speaker Reed, opposed the conquest of the Philippines, defying the policy of their government, their party, their friends. They had their reward in imposing on the conquest the spirit of freedom; in 1941–2 the United States had *its* reward in the trust and confidence of the Filipinos in the moment of Japanese conquest. Because the United States was a type of political society in which leaders were not reduced to conformity by fear, by uncritical devotion to the "interests of the state," or by worship of the "Bitch-Goddess, Success," the moral bond between conquerors and conquered stood the strain of both being victims, at the same time, of a new conqueror in whose society the mere idea of an opposition like that of the American anti-imperialists was unthinkable and intolerable. And no one planned in 1898 to turn on moral indignation to be used in 1941!

There are permanent dangers, permanent temptations in any imperial policy, in any structure based, even in part, on conquest, on military superiority. But in the free society they are to some extent guarded against by the general political habits of the imperial power. A critic of French society, like André Gide, is helped in his attack on French colonial policy in the Congo by a living French tradition that encourages all such critics of tyranny, French and non-French. When control of the Belgian Congo passed from King Leopold to, in effect, the Belgian Parliament, there was a very rapid improvement of the conditions of the natives. The Belgian voters had both a conscience and a political habit far superior to that of their old king. And the new king, Albert I, was able to play a heroic role in 1914–18, not only because he was a hero but because the Belgian nation had cleansed its hands of the worst sins of Leopold II.

Indeed the point can be made from German history. For if it is debatable whether German colonial methods in Africa were any more brutal than those of the other colonial powers, it is indisputable that they were greatly improved by criticism in the old imperial Reichstag. Socialist, Centre, Liberal criticism improved the administration of the Cameroons, lessened the shame of the Herrero War in South-west Africa, lessened the likelihood of a continuation of the Karl Peters methods in East Africa. Again, however difficult it may be to understand, there were honest English publicists and politicians to whom it was one thing to return the ex-German colonies to a Germany that had institutions like those of William II or Weimar and quite another to return them to the Germany represented by the author of *Mein Kampf* and the editor of the *Stürmer*.

There has been a rapid descent in German political morality since 1914 and the world, suspicious of German egotism in 1914, is ten times more suspicious now. It is for this reason that the propaganda of the Third Reich has been such a miserable failure outside the Third Reich. And as far as it has been a success *inside* the Third Reich, it has been the means of further estranging the German people from the rest of the world, no light matter when it has become certain that there is not the slightest chance that the world is going to be recast on German lines. Of what avail is it for the Dutch agents of the German invaders to keep on bleating that the Dutch people insist on disliking the Germans and ignoring the crimes of England in South Africa in 1900? Those crimes were real, but they were not nearly as great as German crimes—and they were not committed in the midst of an English silence. The incompetence—and worse—of the British concentration camps in South Africa was exposed by a great Englishwoman, member of a typical English political dynasty, Emily Hobhouse. They were denounced at the time by a great Scotsman, Campbell-Bannerman, as "methods of barbarism." Campbell-Bannerman had spent a great part of his political life in the War Office, but he had a more delicate sense of the honour of the British Army than has the average Prussian officer of his honour. In six years' time the man who had so affronted the pride and moral self-esteem of his countrymen was swept into office by the greatest political landslide ever known. And he was not content with his past denunciation of the South African War, he restored full self-government to the old Boer Republics. It is because of Campbell-Bannerman—and the repentance of the British people—that Marshal Smuts has twice been a formidable enemy of the Reich. And more significant still, it was because in the darkest hour of the

Boer people a leading British statesman was found to denounce his own people, that General Botha, the Boer leader, trusted the British Prime Minister. If Campbell-Bannerman, as leader of the Opposition, had not denounced the way the war was conducted, he could not as Prime Minister have made lasting peace.

The great tragedy of American history, the murder of Lincoln by John Wilkes Booth, tells the same story. The murder was the act of a fanatic of the kind in which Germany has been so rich. It meant the end of the possibility of the great American Civil War leaving only quick-healing scars. It meant that, for the moment, the spirit of the Second Inaugural was killed. And what was that spirit? The spirit of a man in the moment of complete military triumph, reflecting on the share of the victors in the origins of the tragedy: "The Almighty has His own purposes. 'Woe unto the world because of offences: for it must needs be that offences come, but woe to that man by whom the offence cometh.' If we shall suppose that American slavery is one of those offences which, in the providence of God must needs come, but which, having continued through His appointed time, He now wills to remove, and that He gives to both North and South this terrible war as the woe due to those by whom the offence come, shall we discern therein any departure from those divine attributes which the believers in a living God always ascribe to him? Fondly do we hope, fervently do we pray, that this mighty scourge of war may speedily pass away. Yet if God wills that it continue until all the wealth piled by the bondsman's two hundred and fifty years of unrequited toil shall be sunk and until every drop of blood drawn with the lash shall be paid by another drawn by the sword, as was said three thousand years ago, so still it must be said: 'The judgments of the Lord are true and righteous altogether.' With malice toward none, with charity for all, with firmness in the right as God gives us to see the right, let us strive on to finish the work we are in, to bind up the nation's wounds, to care for him who shall have borne the battle and for his widow and his orphan, to do all which may achieve and cherish a just and lasting peace among ourselves and with all nations."

The man who spoke like that was killed by a man who would have been at home in the Nazi party. But it was American society and the American way of life that produced Lincoln and put him at the head of the American state and that has since made him the most popular and representative of great Americans. What German leader has ever spoken that way, *in triumph*? What German leader has made a German victory of interest to anybody but Germans? Of course, romantic and unpolitical writers like Carlyle tried to make the German triumph of 1870 a matter of universal pride and gratification, but Bismarck could not speak like Lincoln, still less could William II, and the new triumphant Second Reich found itself like a parvenu millionaire forced to "throw its weight about" to attract attention, and since it was conspicuously not much loved, it decided to be feared.

After the last war there developed a deep misunderstanding between the German people and the Western countries. For the revision of the Treaty of Versailles was discussed in very different moral contexts. To the victorious Western peoples it was not enough to have won, it was necessary to have used the victory in ways according with principles of general justice. But for the German assailants of the treaty there were no such principles when they worked *against* the interests or the pride of Germany. The complaints of injustice were mere tactical devices, a mere case of "making a poor mouth," as they say in Ireland.

The result was a profound disillusionment—for which Germany will have to pay. The Germans (not all by any means Nazi by conviction) who thought the occupation of Prague perfectly right and reasonable, failed to understand the shock given in the West to the whole system based on a belief in a common standard of political morality. The rights of nations, used so vigorously up to Munich, were dropped as soon as they served their purpose. The destruction of the Polish state, the degradation of the Polish people, with no very vigorous protest from any representative Germans, like the unnameable infamies committed against the Jews, have made very many people in the Western world wonder if the German people are *politically* capable of civilization. The silence of Cardinal Innitzer of Vienna, when the Third Reich set out to degrade the whole Polish nation, awakened some interesting reflections, both on the long record of clerical servility in Austria and on that great event in the history of Vienna, the rescue of the city from the Turks by a Polish army under King John Sobieski. And those who remembered it may well have reflected that the battle-cry of the Polish king ("Not unto us, O Lord, but to Thy Name give the glory") was not the kind of invocation of God or Providence that modern Germany had made familiar to the world.

And another and not minor barrier between Germany and the West, is the odious nature of the exploitation of Norwegian charity. That those Austrian children whom Norwegian families had taken to save from starvation should return as invaders, chosen because they knew the country and the language *and should expect to be welcomed*, that is an example of exploitation of old friends which is one of the great political mistakes that come from the naïve politics of picking up quick tricks by any means! Professional soldiers in the West think that it is a military weakness too, that the Marne, Stalingrad, the collapse of the offensives of 1918, the failure in Normandy, all illustrate an inability not to snatch quick minor advantages that have later to be paid for. It is possible that the same naïve views of the nature of reality are at fault.

And that naïve view is egotistic. It is egotistic in the endless autobiographical speeches of the Führer, in the endless recapitulation of his wrongs and triumphs, the hysterical denunciation of the hydra-headed foe, the pathological identification of the German people with himself and of himself with Providence. There is none of the humour, even occasional humility, that in the Western peoples leads to real self-criticism and even to occasional repentance of their *own* national sins. There is none of that respect for the individual dissenter from the national current passion that led the beleaguered people of Charleston, during the American Civil War, to honour in life and death their great fellow-citizen, Hugh Legaré, who knew—and said—that they were wrong. There is no equivalent

B*

in German history for that long list of British dissenters from the current passions of the nation whom the nation has yet honoured. When the old English aristocratic state was at its height of glory and success in the long war against Napoleon, the Imperator (as Treitschke calls him) had his admirers in the highest circles of that society. He had his defenders among men of genius like Hazlitt and the picture of the Corsican Ogre painted by one set of British writers and talkers was countered by a less passionate view taken by others. Great national figures like Byron were bitter critics of the treatment of Marshal Ney; great noblemen like Lord Holland made the treatment of Napoleon at St. Helena one of the main wrongs against which they fought. Men of genius and talent after the last war made the wrongs, real or alleged, of Germany *their* main cause. But there has been no equivalent German movement of repentance in Germany for wrongs done to Poles, to Jews, to the victims of the Third Reich or indeed of the Second. When we contrast the action of the Belgian rulers of Louvain University, refusing to permit the new library to bear an inscription recalling who had destroyed the old, with the incessant recapitulation of German grievances from 1918 to 1939 by all parties in Germany, we are forced to wonder if there is not lacking in German social education some of the necessary elements of self-criticism and proportion that the West has slowly and expensively acquired. When we remember the way in which the great festivals in honour of the re-opening of Rheims Cathedral in 1937 were *not* made the occasion of recrimination against the nation that had wrecked so much and when we think of the cultivation of the resentments of the Germans over the Ruhr, we seem to be contrasting an adult with a childish society. At best, we are only seeing a new example of the bitter truth laid down by an English poet:

> "Forgiveness to the injured does belong;
> But they ne'er pardon, who have done the wrong."

It is childish, too, to rate too highly the controversial method beloved of children: "You're another." For in the Western tradition there are plenty of people to agree, but not to accept the conclusion that sins and errors cancel out. It is easy to find grounds for accusing American and British society of a race prejudice not very different from that which makes injustice, robbery, and murder none of these things if done by Germans to Jews or Poles. But in British and American societies there are always people to say that they *are* sins and slowly, painfully, to reduce the areas in which they are practised or palliated. American slavery was a great sin. But it is to be noted that the most conclusive evidence of this comes from Americans. "Can the liberties of a nation be thought secure when we have removed their only firm basis, a conviction in the minds of the people that these liberties are the gift of God? That they are not to be violated but with His wrath? Indeed, I tremble for my country when I reflect that God is just; that His justice cannot sleep forever. . . . The Almighty has no attribute which can take sides with us in such a contest." The writer of this prophetic passage was Thomas Jefferson, a President of the United States and a slave-owner. But he did not seek to be deceived. Lynching is a most odious crime; it has been widely practised but it has not been erected into a system of government. And the spectacle of John Jay Chapman making a private pilgrimage to a town where such a national crime had been committed, to make what personal expiation he could of the crime, is a spectacle which, in the strict sense of the term, is edifying. It would be edifying too if we had a German example, if any German of Chapman's class had gone to expiate Prussian oppression of the Polish people in Posznan, if, in the future, any leading German professor went to expiate there the planting of that short-lived weed, the Nazi university of Posen.

In the old days when Germany was not cutting herself off in her new pride and prosperity from the West, such repentance was not unknown. The average German was not proud of the Prussian record in Poland; although even then there were traces of national egotism in such products of the German philosophical schools as Karl Marx. When Bismarck bought Russian support by turning over Polish patriots to the Tsar, there were plenty of Germans to protest at the high price. But victory in 1866 and 1870 began that estrangement from the common code of international decency which by blinding the German people to the realities of the world, moral as well as physical, has conducted them twice to disaster.

Only the most foolish American and English talkers and writers fail to see and to talk of the many dark stains on the national record. Only the most naïve Dutch defenders of the Dutch imperial record defend the past exploitation of Java. And in France, the danger to French liberty and, indeed, decency caused by the bad habits learned by French officers in the African wars, was a commonplace of French political literature all through the nineteenth century. In India, it is mainly with British political weapons that British rule is fought. It is easier, to-day, to find British readers for books like E. M. Forster's *A Passage to India* than to find acceptance for the doctrines of Kipling.

The habit of self-criticism, of repentance, is inbred in the Western societies. It is not merely on an "honesty is the best policy" basis that the British Government and people have refused to break the treaty agreement made with Ireland in 1938, the agreement that, by depriving the British Navy of the use of the Irish ports, made the risks of a German triumph so much greater. It was not merely to impress on the neutral world the contrast with Germany (for who could doubt that in comparable circumstances the Third Reich would have secured the bases by the usual methods of a guarantee of a non-aggression pact followed, in months or years, with an invasion, complete with documents to show that the lamb was about to attack the lion?). It was largely because the British people had a bad record and a bad conscience and, slowly accepting these facts—at great immediate risk—decided to have no more on its conscience. That the war has been won anyway, that this decision has been politically wise, should not detract from the importance of the decision of 1940-1. It was simply a proof of the sincerity with which the British and American peoples accept the dogma that "righteousness exalteth a nation." That righteousness may be often hidden, may be only a source of action from time to time, but if the German people cannot accept the fact that one of the lubricants that makes the free system of the West work, is a belief in a general political morality that indeed pays, but is not obeyed only when it pays or because it pays, they will again fail to understand what the Western victors think of the world and be incapable of re-entering that Western culture from which, for three generations past, they have been more and more determinedly exiling themselves.

CHAPTER TWO

CASE FOR POLITICS

I

IN contemplating, however briefly, the devices by which the ideal of the free state is given necessarily imperfect embodiment, we must beware of taking too seriously the frequently contemptuous language in which the success of these devices and the morality and skill of their manipulators is spoken of in old free societies. It would be foolish to take too seriously the anti-clerical language of deeply religious; peoples and even the verbal contempt of deeply political peoples for politics and politicians is no sufficient basis on which to build a system of anti-democratic government. The role of the politician is in some ways ungrateful. Just because the task to which he sets his hand is so difficult, so indispensable, so great in the claims made on its behalf, it has often provoked a critical discontent which, when more than merely verbal, expresses the discontent of the citizen with the contrast between the highness of the target aimed at and the moderate level of success of the marksmen. Subjects of an absolute state find it easier to experience the felicity promised to those that expect little because they shall not be disappointed. The "Good Duke Alfred" of *South Wind* did, it is not impossible, win from his subjects genuine gratitude for not behaving worse. And there may have been many Hanoverians who really thought Ernest I a true father of his people. Certainly no free society could get as much gratitude for as little effort as kings and princes have been always given by courtiers and flatterers, who are the public opinion of absolute states. When we have to admit that in any free state some or most of the politicians are regarded with tolerant scepticism, we should note that one of the benefits sought by the free state is the creation of tolerance and the encouragement of scepticism about the infallibility and even the *ex officio* probity of rulers. There is, in the democratic ideal, a combination of faith in the general wisdom of mankind with doubt that its great limitations have been removed from any individual or group. The case against the Roman *optimates*, or the American Federalists, "good, wise, and rich," is less that they doubted of the political wisdom and probity of the masses, than that they had a totally uncritical faith in their own wisdom and uprightness. There is nothing more naïve than a fashion of condemning politicians which is not the expression of a generally rigid political and private morality, applied to Church *and* State, the arts and business, soldiers and philosophers alike. Only the anarchist is entitled to such severity of judgment and the anarchist, the practical anarchist that is, is not in question here. Theoretical anarchy, contempt for *all* authority, combined with practical obedience to *any* authority, is an intellectual luxury often covering political laziness. It opens the way to any type of authority that can make the grade and it is not specifically anti-democratic. Even if the people is an incompetent tyrant, from this point of view are not all authorities tyrannical and discussion of their relative degrees of sin and folly a waste of breath? Western free government, so long established, so materially successful, so kind to anarchists, is surely as good, from this point of view, as any other form of rule?

The fact that politicians are not usually saints, not often men of genius and seldom wholly trusted, is accepted. "You cannot fool all of the people all of the time," said a very eminent politician, and Lincoln was far from reproaching any free people for this recurrent scepticism. But because it was believed in the Middle Ages that an archdeacon could not save his soul, there was no movement to abolish the necessary officer all the same.[1] And although sceptical fighting soldiers, in all armies, have made fun of staff officers, of their cowardice and incom-

[1] Two archdeacons, Thomas Becket and Hildebrand, were canonized. St. Thomas of Canterbury and St. Gregory VII, it should be remembered, were political saints, canonized for political action. A non-political Pope, the Celestine V damned by Dante, was so condemned for refusing the dangerous sanctity of politics. He, like some nations, made *per viltà, il gran rifiuto*.

petence, they are necessary all the same. So are even very mediocre politicians, who are only to be condemned for not meeting the standards of their art, not for not being hermits, or poets, or makers of symmetrical systems of political practice and morality. Their pattern is not one laid up in heaven and the less they think of their own footsteps as resembling those of an audible divine purpose the better. Their duty is not to meet the specifications laid down by Plato or Hegel, but the endless, varied and unpredictable demands of situations created by varied human wills working with this recalcitrant material universe to produce improvement by tolerably honest and dignified methods.[1]

"A statesman is a dead politician," said an American living politician, and there is this much of truth in the dictum that all statesmen in free societies are and must be politicians. When Gladstone announced that he was "an old parliamentary hand," he was stating one of his necessary qualifications for being in his life and death a statesman.[2] The only alternatives are being courtiers, demagogues or conspirators. Yet the old literary prejudice against the politician remains, not very harmful in free states but harmful there, too, since it encour-

[1] In Prince-ruled Germany, the politician had no very good name either. But the different meaning given to the word is significant of the different historical experience of the German people, which has important consequences in 1944. "Law was important for future rulers and officials, and 'politics' in the special sense attached to the word then, was of value to all. It meant the art of self-advancement by 'finesse' and civility, the 'suaviter in modo' praised by Lord Chesterfield. The 'politic' man or 'Politikus' who figures so largely in literature at the beginning of the century, is the master of the 'lesser talents,' whose *savoir-vivre* wins him favour with the great." (Bruford, *Germany in the Eighteenth Century*, p. 68.) It is worth noting that Chesterfield's son, on whom political advice of this level was lavished, was found, in fact, to be only fit to be a minor English diplomat in Germany. He was totally unfit for real political life.

[2] The historical context of this famous joke should be noted. It was made when Gladstone had decided to introduce a bill giving Home Rule for Ireland, a decision that he knew might wreck his party and his power. (It did.) No decision has ever been more morally creditable to a great statesman. (How unthinkable is the idea of Bismarck or any other German statesman running any risk to do justice to the Poles of Posen or Polish Pomerania!)

ages the political laziness of bad citizens and provides weapons for the apologists for the non-free solution of the problem of state life. What is the case against the politician? In some of the most famous satirical verses in English poetry the case against the politician, at any rate against the politician of genius, is put with force. To Oliver Goldsmith, the spectacle of his fellow-Irishman, Edmund Burke, wasting on mere politics such prodigious literary talents, was as irritating as to a German lover of poetry was the spectacle of Goethe appearing to waste on the petty problems of Saxe-Weimar the time and energy that might have produced another *Faust*. The non-political talents were there all right. Had not Burke as a young man written that essay on *The Sublime and the Beautiful* which Lessing began to translate and which did for the author of *Laocoön* what Hume did for Kant? No one can read Burke without being impressed by the mere literary talent, rhetorical and argumentative genius, spent on what may seem to be transitory topics. If the legend be true that Burke was a candidate for the chair of Moral Philosophy in Glasgow University which was won by Adam Smith, that university lost a great professor. From the very beginning Burke was seen by the most critical contemporaries as a great man. Charles Fox and Dr. Johnson agreed on that. Yet he was content to be a not very successful orator in the House of Commons; was content to serve as the "brains trust," to use a modern term, for a series of mediocre aristocratic politicians. Was not Goldsmith right to lament such a misplaced use of talents.

> "Here lies our good Edmund, whose genius was such,
>   We scarcely can praise it, or blame it too much;
>   Who, born for the Universe, narrow'd his mind,
>   And to party gave up what was meant for mankind."

The answer is "no." The purely scientific genius, the poet who is, above all else, a poet, will not betray science or poetry for politics. If he tries to do so his divided mind will reveal itself and cripple his political career, driving him back to his real vocation. But a society in which the political life and the art of politics are only pursued by the mediocre, is an unhealthy society and the waste of genius on politics, if waste there be, is part of the price to be paid for the rewards of the free society, rewards shared in by the man of genius who gives up to politics what was meant, possibly, for art. Some of the men who have made this sacrifice have been conscious that it was a sacrifice. Jefferson who, for variety of aptitudes, was Goethe's compeer as well as contemporary, explained his refusal to undertake literary work for which he seemed so well fitted. It was after his retirement from the presidency that he was forced to say: "While in public life I had not the time, and now that I am retired I am past the time."[1]

Cicero, Demosthenes, Thucydides, Machiavelli, Milton, Polybius, these are great mén who played a part in politics. And the power of their literary work was made possible, in great part, by their first-hand knowledge of politics. It is true of *Paradise Lost* as well as of *The Prince*. (German equivalents are harder to find, but Goethe's role as chief minister of the tiny state of Saxe-Weimar did him no harm.)

But it will be objected, it was not to the nation but to *party* that Burke gave up what was meant for mankind. It was, and it is, one of the greatest achievements of Burke that he won the argument in this case against Goldsmith, against Bolingbroke, and against all the purists of politics, then and since, to whom the necessary compromises of politics, the necessary tolerances of party politics are intolerable, usually more for aesthetic than strictly moral reasons. In a free society it is only by sacrificing to party that the nation can be served. Such a sacrifice is real, but so are the sacrifices imposed by any art.

But before we consider the sacrifices made by politicians to

[1] Jefferson's self-chosen epitaph may seem to some to show contempt for his political career. It lists only three achievements. It does not mention that Jefferson had been President, Vice-President, Secretary of State, Governor of Virginia, Minister to France. But the three things for which Jefferson wished to be remembered were, in fact, political achievements. The authorship of the Declaration of Independence, the authorship of the Virginia Statute for Religious Freedom are obviously political. But so was the founding of the University of Virginia of which Jefferson wished to be remembered as the "Father." For the most important function of the University of Virginia was to be a school of politics.

party—and their justification—it is necessary to consider some other charges against the class. They are accused, often, of pursuing only mediocre objects, of being followers rather than leaders. "I must follow them, I am their leader," said Ledru-Rollin in defence of some foolish action. This charge is, in fact, that the leader in a democracy must flatter the mob as a courtier must flatter the prince. If the mob, if the voters were as capable of perpetual attention to the siren songs of flattery, the state of the free world would not be much better than that of the tyrant's world. But it is not, in fact, as bad. For in the tyrant's world flattery is either upwards only, as when only the will of the prince need be considered, or it is mutual. A modern demagogic tyrant like Hitler or Mussolini is both an exporter and importer of flattery on a great scale. Mussolini told the Italians they were Ancient Romans, while they were both better and worse; Hitler told the Germans they were a *Herrenvolk* of technically advanced barbarians and did his best to make his flattery the truth. In return, the only permitted mouthpieces of the Italian and German peoples poured out on the tyrants flattery that would have startled a satrap of a Persian king, or the king himself. It is evident from the recent history of the world, that the abolition of free institutions is no cure for demogogic flattery; it makes it a two-way traffic—to the disastrous loss of each party.

A democratic politician is often tempted to play up to his voters by assuring them of an admiration for their wisdom that he cannot always feel. But he cannot flatter *all* the voters successfully; even if he wins, there is a minority who are sceptical as far as he is concerned and that minority is not absolutely certain to remain a minority. His rivals, too, have means of persuading the voters that they have been deceived (not necessarily creditable means). The object of the flattery is not a unit; there is competition in the courting of the voters and, most important of all, the voters have more reasons for scepticism than have the princes and tyrants. The painful corrective of facts is always at hand. In the English story King Canute rebukes his servile courtiers who had told him all things obeyed him. The tide did not, and the king got his feet wet.

The people often gets its feet wet and, it may be suggested, knows that it well may. The prince may never have the chastening experience of taking the advice of a flatterer and finding that things go wrong in a way immediately painful to him. The cost of the error is borne by others. At worst, the people is an unorganized court; the daily incense that floats up into the nostrils of all rulers whose authority is unquestionable, is only from time to time offered the sovereign people. "You will never hear the truth or eat a bad dinner again," so in the Catholic clerical joke, a priest addresses a new-made bishop. But the people will eat many very bad dinners, will at times have to go without dinner, and the memory and anticipation of this risk ensures that there is more democratic scepticism than mere inspection of election addresses suggests. There is always the minority to say, "I told you so." (Who so addresses the tyrant?) And there are, in any real free state, many more instruments for winning the ear of the people than are at the disposal of the most unscrupulous politician. Cleon, in ancient Athens, had only to win over the Assembly; the men who have the *entrée* to the court of the dictator have only to win him. But in a modern democracy there are so many competing voices, so many views that may be for the moment disregarded but which cannot be silenced and will, if things go wrong, be remembered!

Another charge often brought against the politician is his lack of genuine faith. Contrast, we are told, the passion, the vigour, with which X denounces Y and predicts from the success of his policy, the ruin of the state. Yet if Y wins, X congratulates him and does not commit suicide rather than see the inevitable downfall of his country. In a few years' time he may even replace Y at the head of the state. If it has not been visibly ruined he does not apologize for his prophecies; if it is in a bad way he does not demand the head of Y, who is covered by the mandate given him by the sovereign people. On this view all party politics are a comedy; all democratic politics are only a game. In the West, there is no Germanic passion for tragedy for tragedy's sake and no distaste for comedy. Yet there is an element of truth in the criticism; the plain man may be puzzled by the apparent hypocrisy of the politicians. The hypocrisy is often merely formal; the language of elections is no more to be taken literally than the servile formulas of polite correspondence. A politician in the democratic West who lives on mere rhetoric does not, as a rule, live well. And, all questions of popular discrimination apart, the politician in the free society has to work with other politicians. Even if he is a Prime Minister, he has to submit to questioning in the House of Commons, to answer speeches which may be malignant, may be foolish, may be brilliant and unscrupulous rhetorical performances—or be serious statements that deserve, as well as need, an answer. A President of the United States cannot order Congress about; he can only speak to it in person or appeal over its head to the common master, the People of the United States. And Congress or members of Congress can speak too. The President of the United States submitting to questioning at a press conference, the Prime Minister of England scoring off a questioner by wit and good temper, these are great officers being educated in their human limitations. Of course, in nine cases out of ten, it is a waste of their time and the national time; but the fact that there is a tenth time is decisive; it reminds them, as Cromwell reminded the Scotch ministers who had their divine intuition, that they may be wrong. Unfortunately, there was no effective organ to remind a military dictator like Cromwell that *he* could be wrong.

And among the numerous things that convinced the pacific, complacent, lazy, free peoples of the West that war with Nazi Germany was inevitable, was the radio that brought the noise and temper of a *Parteitag* home to people who were very reluctant to believe that, politically speaking, Germany was a retarded nation. Those yells, those screams of "Sieg Heil," these were good enough for a football game, but that was all. But above all, the Führer's manner, his voice, his complete disregard of all the civilized decencies of argument and temper, these were most powerful calls to vigilance. This was another, and unpolitical, world, in which the head of a great state could speak in a manner that would have disgraced a drunken candidate for a minor office. And who can doubt that had Hitler had to undergo the discipline of a parliament, he would have been either totally discredited or made more formally civilized? Those endless assertions of untruths, that tireless recapitulation of past wrongs, this dream-world of hate and megalomania, these were products of a political career never submitted to political discipline, the discipline of submitting to the critical attention of colleagues. For one most valuable corrective to the temptations of the demagogue is to have to try to repeat, in Parliament or Congress, the easy successes of the mass meeting. In a free society, unless that success can be repeated, there is no real success. And the mere rhetoric that is sometimes adequate for the public meeting is never adequate for the organized assembly that has heard that kind of thing before and has other more critical and, if you like, more cynical standards. It may be a pity that democratic leaders should greet each other like Roman Augurs, with difficulty repressing a smile, but it is better that they should be cynical than that they should be victims of their self-induced hysteria.[1]

The apparent contrast between the fervour of the masses and the cynicism of their elected representatives is naturally a frequent subject of angry or ironical comment in free states. "There is more in common," said Robert de Jouvenel, "between two deputies, one of whom is a revolutionary, than two revolutionaries, one of whom is a deputy." It is a pity if the political habits of a country are such that the verbal violence of electoral language is such that this dictum is true. Yet it may be doubted if the French electors who sent Pierre Laval to Parliament really thought him as dangerous a revolutionary as he professed, verbally, to be. There is in all politics something of the conventions of opera. And if democratic politicians are too tolerant of each other, is the opposite weakness to be cultivated? If political conflict is not pushed to the edge of

[1] Of all the Nazi leaders, the only one who could, I think, have had a serious political career in a free society is Goebbels. His talents are of a kind for which there is a market on the margin of democratic politics, where rabble-rousing journalism and bogus radicalism meet. He could even have been a columnist of a common enough type. He could have risen to a not very creditable place in the third rank of democratic politicians.

unforgivable offences and unbridgeable breaches, is that to be deplored? Did the Roman Republic show more signs of political health when the incompetent demagogue Consul, after the disaster of Cannae, was congratulated by his senatorial enemies because he had not despaired of the Republic, or when its political history became a series of bloody proscriptions in which victors and vanquished alike played double or quits? For if it *is* double or quits, if there is no possible retreat, if the whole destiny of the nation has been taken into one pair of hands, then the dictator and his colleagues must play double or quits, for there is no way out for them.

The distinction between dangerous complaisance and wise magnanimity is hard to draw but it must be drawn. Yet a nation is fortunate that can say:

> "In diesen heil'gen Hallen,
> Kennt man die Rache nicht,
> Und ist ein Mensch gefallen
> Führt Liebe ihn zur Pflicht."

To think well of one's fellow citizens till positive proof of treason or corruption is given, is the highest political wisdom. A system kept going only by "nights of the long knives" has no health in it.

And it must not be assumed that the professional politician has not some of the qualities of his defects. He may and, indeed, must sacrifice a great deal of intellectual symmetry; he must cultivate patience until it almost ceases to be a virtue (though this is not likely to be thought a fault for a long time, in a Europe that has known so many catastrophes arising from the Führer's announcements that *his* patience was exhausted). He must remember, all the time, that he is dealing with men who are no more fools than he is. This, if no higher motive is at work, saves him from certain suicidal forms of cunning. In all probability, the Führer himself and certainly vast numbers of Germans, never appreciated the working of the law of diminishing returns as applied to promises. To break one promise and immediately to offer the victim an even more lavish and oath-buttressed promise was a trick that worked the first time. "But a lie can never be young but once." Probably Hitler never understood the effect on the American people of solemn promises of good will accompanied by arguments that, in any case, it was not in Germany's immediate interest to attack the United States or threaten the Americas. The Americas wanted a world in which promises were kept even after it was to the interest of the promiser to break them—and had not enough confidence in the Führer's wisdom to take comfort in the thought that, at the moment, he could see no profit in open action against America. No politician who had risen the hard way, by the democratic process of convincing *somebody* that there was a real community of interest, even of low interest, would have made this mistake.

In the United States, and even in more decorous and less candid England, there is an agreement among political commentators that one saving virtue of a politician is that he usually keeps his word. A politician who does not, who for any reason gets the reputation of being untrustworthy, suffers an intolerable handicap. He may, like Shelburne, be so distrusted by all parties that his great talents and other forms of political virtue may do him or his country little good. He may find that after a brief moment of exhilarating triumph, the rest of his life is spent in shallows and in miseries with lesser men preferred to power. "An honest politician is a man who, when bought, stays bought." Such is the worldly doctrine attributed to an American practitioner.

"Put not your trust in princes," says Holy Writ, but princes and dictators tend to think themselves above the necessity of being reliable. So instead of party conflicts and compromises, even that less dignified form of compromise, a deal, they get obedience or conspiracy. For even in a court or dictatorial clique, the lesson of the common life must be learned. "Had Zimri peace that slew his master?" Had Hitler peace that slew his servants again and again and was forced to the last argument of dictators, death?

The politician, for all the faults his trade breeds in him, is a necessity; his professional deformation has to be accepted like the corresponding professional distortions that mark priests, soldiers, doctors, or other practitioners of difficult arts. Mere anti-clericalism, mere anti-militarism is not enough; neither is mere exposure of the weaknesses and corruptions of politics and politicians.

The politician is a bargainer, a man who serves his country best when he finds a day-to-day solution of the competing claims of classes, individuals, experts, amateurs, problems seen to be urgent by all, problems seen to be urgent by few, problems that are real, problems that are fictitious. He is a distributor of priorities, a harmonizer of claims to priorities. For there is no scheme laid down in the nature of things which makes it clear to every right-minded man what is to be done *now*. At a few moments in national history there may be only one problem, survival; but even that raises questions of means. And survival once attained, what is to be done with the state is a question that demands especially urgent answers after the ordeal of a great war.

It is an error, not confined to Germany but very common in Germany, that there can be a science of government, that it is a field of *expertise* to be cultivated by the experts. But this superstition of the *Fachmann* leads, in fact, to the elevation to the power of final decision of far more irresponsible amateurs than a democratic policy elevates to power. There are no universal experts; there is no training that is valid for all the fields of decision that must be cultivated by the rulers of a modern state; some people must specialize in non-specialism, that is be politicians. All that remains is to find out what kind of politicians do least harm and some good.

It is obviously untrue that human beings in any country are neatly divided into two groups, one holding "advanced" and the other "conservative" views. Some people who are politically "advanced" are very conservative in cultural and other points, even on some political points. Some conservatives are free (except in politics) from conservative bias. Nevertheless, there is a temperament that welcomes change, and a temperament that resists it and the division into "Left" and "Right," if not taken too rigidly, is yet not meaningless. In the English-speaking world at any rate, if you know that a man is a vegetarian, totally or semi-pacifist, devoted to new movements in the arts and hostile to old-fashioned educational methods, you are usually right in putting him in the Left camp. And the social conservative, the *laudator temporis acti*, in sport, weather, manners, is usually politically conservative too.

More people than Gilbert's philosophical guardsman have been of his somewhat puzzled mind:

> "I always think it comical
> How Nature always does contrive
> That every boy and every girl,
> That's born into the world alive,
> Is either a little Liberal,
> Or else a little Conservative."

But if the contrivance is not wholly nature's doing, it is partly nature's doing and that is why art has been able to create those odd structures, the two-party systems of Britain and the United States. Whether the two-party system existed in Burke's time, whether he was a historian or a prophet, it came to exist.

What is the main object and the main justification of the two-party system, the political system dominant in the two great states which have had the longest continuous history as free states? It is governmental. "The King's government must be carried on," said the Duke of Wellington. To translate this into realistic terms it is necessary that the English voters should be able to rely on there being always in existence a group of men adequately known to the public by past behaviour and current promise, more or less united in general political bias, some of them, at least, with past experience of the realities of government. This group is the *Opposition*; the Administration, the Cabinet, is a group of the same kind but, from the point of view of the free state, it is the existence of the Opposition that is most important. For it means that the Government cannot play the dictatorial trick of putting the nation into the impossible position of having no alternative Government, of forcing conspiracy on ill-prepared generals and revolt on ill-equipped peoples. "There are no necessary men" is a democratic slogan that can only be confidently asserted where the alternative to rule by the men in power is always ready. In the United States, there is the same justification in slightly different institutional form. Because power in the American system is much less concentrated than in the English, it is less necessary to organize an Opposition that is a "shadow cabinet." But it *is* necessary to see that the divided instruments of power, the Presidency, the Senate, the House of Representatives, the Supreme Court, are not in the gift of any one man, or group, that the sovereign voter has at least a minimum of choice in his revolt against the "never-ending audacity of elected persons," to quote a great democratic poet, Walt Whitman.

It is to secure the availability of a united alternative government in the English cabinet system, to secure that the President of the United States (who cannot, obviously, be divided) shall be the preferred choice of the majority of the American people, shall be a national embodiment of the will and power of "WE, the People of the United States," that so much is sacrificed to party unity. That much is sacrificed should be admitted at once; that much is gained must now be shown.

The first thing that is gained is the imposition of responsibility on both parties. On the Government, there is imposed the responsibility of so running the state that the Opposition will not have its task of winning an election made farcically easy. On the Opposition there is imposed the responsibility of not making its own task of government impossible when it comes into power. This being so, it is bad for a free state to have anything like the politics of a one-party state. If one party is so obviously dominant that it has no real fear of defeat, its sense of responsibility may be reduced to next to nothing; if the other party has no hope of success it may as well have its verbal fling, promise heaven and threaten hell without having the fear of having to govern a country in a state more like purgatory.

In a free state this condition is abnormal but not impossible. Historical accident, the passions of civil war for example, may so anchor certain parts of the country to a party name that real opposition to the owners of the party name is impossible.

Religious divisions reflected in political divisions may produce the same result. Since the relative strength of religious denominations does not easily change, parties based on them remain remarkably stable, as is the case in Holland and was the case in pre-Hitler Germany. But it should be noted that it is very unlikely that in a free state, a *majority* party can be so constituted. Religious parties like those of the Catholics in Holland or pre-Hitler Germany are in their nature minority parties; a country in which the religious majority has to organize its political life on purely religious lines is a most unlikely phenomenon.

But historical tradition may produce purely historical voting. The classical example is the effect of the Civil War in the United States which anchored all of the South to the Democratic party and a great part of the North to the Republican party. To some degree, this historical situation created, in parts of the United States, the evils of the one-party state. In mild forms, for no party had an automatic control of the federal government nor indeed was there any guarantee that the same party would control *all* sections of the federal government. Therefore the worst extravagances and abuses of the totalitarian one-party state were avoided. But the lesser evils of the one-party state existed. It was not, and is not, an accident, as Virginius Dabney has pointed out, that it is in the South with a one-party system based on a race conflict that the worst demagogues and the most ill-bred political extravagances are commonest.

But in nothing has the practical political genius of the American people been more clearly shown than in their solution of this problem over the greater part of the Union. Since so many Americans, showing that very historical feeling (normally a national asset, but here a liability) refused to vote for any but the candidates who bore the label of the historical party they adhered to, the law accepted this fact. It accepted it—and restored free choice—by the device of the primary. In the primary election the American voter chooses freely who of any number of aspirants shall be the (Republican or Democratic) candidate. Thus the worst evils of the one-party system are avoided, for they inhere in the *Führerprinzip*, in the devolution of party authority *downward* from the top. A one-party system in which authority is conferred on the leaders from the bottom, in which an old party leader is replaced by a new-comer when the electors want to change, in which, indeed, the party label only means that the candidate has been chosen by a majority of the people who have chosen to call themselves Democrats or Republicans for that occasion, is not a one-party system at all; it is simply a complicated system of democratic choice. The primary makes the career of the mere party *Bonzen*, the manipulators of the party machine, more difficult. It makes such pathological parodies of parties as the "monolithic" Nazi party impossible. It provides facilities for checking any tendency of party leaders to think themselves inspired and it frees the rank and file from the pressure of any party conformity except to the party label—which the rank and file themselves confer.

II

The power of the plain man to accept—and to refuse to accept—claims to leadership is secured (imperfectly, of course; life is like that) both by a lively party system and by systems like the primary that promote lively contests inside the party. And these contests ensure what is one of the most important successes of any system of government, that the transfer of the executive and legislative power from one group to another shall be made regularly, peaceably, and with the moral authority that attaches to the working of a national institution, not the mere claim to obedience that comes from the successful exercise or seizure of force. More and more this strength of the free state has been illustrated by the weakness of its rivals, especially that form of authoritarian government exemplified by fascist régimes, in Italy or Germany. One most important thing *they* cannot do is to ensure that their "thousand-year régimes" will last beyond the life of their founders.

The apologists for tyranny always argue as if the tyrant were immortal. Even if we ignore the fact that quite often the tyrant outlives his tyranny, we can hardly ignore the fact that he does, in the more or less long run, die. And no means has been found for the safe, regular transmission of the personal power of a tyrant. He need not be unpopular; he need not have an organized opposition to fear, or an organized system of rivals to manage. But the fact remains that supreme power, if not institutionalized, if not in some way made subject to law, excites appetites, fears, hopes, in a way that no regular succession of power, even of absolute power, does. Indeed the political writers of the eighteenth century discriminated really absolute monarchies from legal monarchies, in this way. A really absolute monarch (a Tsar of Russia, for instance) could alter the succession, could make anybody he liked his heir; thus Peter the Great was able to leave the throne to his widow, a foreigner of very obscure origin. Thus the conspirators who put Catherine II on the throne were able to murder Peter III and put his German widow in power, not as regent for her son, but in her own "right." Louis XIV was not absolute in this sense. The supreme power that he wielded was only his for his lifetime; he could not alter the fundamental laws of the succession. His will could not survive the grave.

Napoleon was clear in his own mind about the difficulty. He could not afford to admit defeat, as the Emperor of Austria or the King of Prussia did. His power was personal, not institutional. In vain he married a Hapsburg and had an heir; in vain he made his brothers kings; in vain he invented a hereditary nobility, a "Conservative Senate." When it was rumoured that he had died in Russia, General Mallet was able to seize the War Ministry; nobody, as Napoleon noted, automatically transferred allegiance to the King of Rome. Who knows or cares what the official succession in the Nazi hierarchy may be? The system dies with the Führer. What a light on the nature of tyranny was thrown by the simple arrest of Mussolini! In an hour, the whole baseless fabric of the corporate state, like an unsubstantial pageant, faded. And in Vichy the lesson was learned, the Marshal sent to Paris for constitutional lawyers to find a constitutional way of retreat.

It is an old story. To found a lasting dynasty was the aim, the never attained aim, of the Greek tyrant in the great ages of Greece. Only when liberty was dead and oriental habits had destroyed the old Greek dignity, was it possible for the successors of Alexander to found hereditary monarchies—which was more than Alexander could do. His infant son might have inherited the throne of Macedonia, but the throne of the Persian kings was no safe seat for a child, though his father had been hailed as a God in his lifetime. The Roman Empire faced and failed to solve the problem. The sacred dignity of the house of Caesar in the East, its military and political prestige in the West, postponed for two generations the violent solution of the problem. But the problem remained; with the suicide of Nero the brutal reality was revealed; the armies made and unmade emperors; it mattered nothing that they did not belong to the divine Julio-Claudian house. They could command the legions. It was impossible to put the supreme power in the hands

of one man, above the laws, above all of the old republican
institutions, the Senate and the People and, at the same time,
to hope to make the throne above illegal competition, to make
law supreme at one part and at one part only of the political
structure, the top.

The conflict may be postponed; it may take the form of
internal struggles, conducted in the corridors or palaces and
in the cells of prisons. The world may only see the signs of
the struggle in a few executions or suicides. The nominal
victor may be dragged from behind the curtains by the
triumphant pretorians, as was Claudius. The real controller
of the supreme state power may take years to secure all
the levers of command and may, for long, refuse the open
honours of his state, but absolute controlled power in the
hands of one man, without legal or traditional checks, cannot
be regularized, cannot be transferred. The dictator may
die in his bed like Gomez of Venezuela; he may die in exile
like Diaz of Mexico. He may attempt, with the spell once
broken, to stage a come-back, announce his conversion to
constitutional monarchy, as Napoleon did in the Hundred
Days that ended at Waterloo, or proclaim the Social Republic, like Mussolini, when he had been rescued by Hitler.
But Humpty Dumpty, once down, is down for ever. And even
if the final catastrophe is avoided, if the tyrant survives to the
end to enjoy his tyranny, it dies with him and has to be remade by a successor whom he may or may not approve of,
whose very name he may not know. Tyranny, the *Führerprinzip*, is the mule of politics, without pride of ancestry or hope
of posterity. Such a system cannot last a thousand years and is
not likely to last fifty. To invite the people of Europe, the heirs
of Jerusalem and Rome and Athens, to accept such a system as
a solution of their political problems, to try to sell this nostrum
to such a market, is to despise the human race even more than
the theories of *Mein Kampf* or the experience of the higher
ranks of the Nazi movement could justify. It *was* put on the
market but it was not bought, not even when the sales talk was
aided by guns and torture. The people of the occupied countries, even the people of Germany, had in their past experience

too goodly a heritage to accept for long this squalid surrender, this substitution of the art of the gangster for the art of the politician. For even had the Führer been a more presentable specimen of his class, had he been a new Augustus, he was not immortal and to accept the rule of the Führer was to take tickets in a lottery in which there might and probably would be more blanks than prizes and might well be no prizes at all. An endless political power game, with guns perpetually on the table, such was the New Europe to which the conquerors invited the conquered. The impossibility of belief that any real organization, stability, coherence was possible under such a system was one of the fatal obstacles to the German attempt at the political exploitation of the victories of 1940. Some of the conquered people might have accepted, with resignation, the apparent verdict of arms, might have accepted the passing of the primacy in Europe to Germany, might have waited for a future in which the conquering people could organize its conquests. But although it was not the only reason for the failure of the New Order, the highly personal and so necessarily unstable character of the new system was one main cause of its failure to win support, except from the venal, terrified and pathological elements of the conquered countries.

Again, it was no new story. Starting with far more advantages, with far more general support, with far less national opposition, with a genuine programme of progress, the French Revolution, as it became personalized in Napoleon, offended more and more people, deceived more and more hopes because its chief, his judgment destroyed by the temptations of personal rule, deprived the subject peoples (and the French people) of any hope of stability. Relying on his military supremacy, he altered frontiers, abolished dynasties, abolished and reformed institutions; he gave nothing time to grow. He could not and did not give the impression of planning beyond his life. It was Europe made and remade according to the caprice of one mortal man who at his back could always hear "time's wingèd chariot hurrying near." The Napoleonic Empire did not last even Napoleon's time any more than the Third Reich's European Empire has lasted Hitler's. Both neglected what Marvell

C

called "the great work of time"—and they were bound to neglect it, for a man who is greater than the institutions of the state he leads cannot build for more than his own brief span and, in effect, does not even attain that limited aim. Not only must the tyrant live in camps and not in cities, erect tents rather than build houses, carry out a nomadic policy, he is tempted, if not forced, to play double or quits. He will not willingly accept limits.

There was, it is true, an old traditional substitute for the regular transfers of authority known in the free state. Hereditary monarchy had the advantage that while its authority was uncontested, the supreme power in the state was not open to competition; it might fall to a child or a semi-moron, but it could not be fought over. And countries tormented by civil war and needing authority above all things, sixteenth-century England and seventeenth-century France, accepted all the drawbacks of putting the supreme power into the arbitrary custody of the workings of heredity as an alternative to anarchy. In Germany, the same movement produced the legalized anarchy of the late Holy Roman Empire with all the disadvantages and, except in the very large states, none of the advantages of hereditary monarchical rule. And while the most important thing to remember about hereditary political authority of this kind is that it is dead as a practical solution, it is not to be forgotten that it has left traces in several countries and most markedly in Germany. They are part of the German bad luck in political matters. What is also to be remembered is that hereditary rule of this kind showed many of the weaknesses of tyrannical rule, though in a less virulent form. We are entitled to notice that Europe has had experience of what it means to be ruled by masters subject to no control from below, masters from whom all power flowed and who were constantly subject, therefore, to great moral and intellectual temptations in the exercise of their functions, though those temptations were far less serious than those that surround an inspired leader who is not limited by education, by tradition, by institutions, and by the knowledge that his birth alone makes him master.

"Power tends to corrupt, and absolute power tends to corrupt absolutely." So wrote John Dalberg Acton, who knew the princely institutions of Germany from the inside (he was a Dalberg) and knew what real political life was too (he was long a Member of Parliament until he was made a peer by his great friend, Gladstone). Power *does* corrupt, but it corrupts the men around the prince as much as it corrupts the prince. And in a court-ridden society only courtiers, this corrupted class, have ready access to the one source of power. It was while the memory of the old court life was still lively that the contempt for its futility was greatest. Cavour, who had first-hand knowledge of what he was talking about, had plenty of support when he declared that "the worst chamber is better than the best ante-chamber."[1]

The strength of the monarchy, even in Germany, decreased without any corresponding diminution in court follies. William I had far more, and far more justified, confidence in his position than had William II, who showed his uneasiness by his theatrical posings, by his demagogic utterances, and by the frivolity of his policy as well as by the worthlessness of his

[1] Again, the very number of courts in Germany ensured that courtiers would be more numerous than elsewhere and, in the tiny states, be even more futile than elsewhere. "It can readily be understood that at every court the suitors for the favour of the prince were as thick as flies round a honey-pot . . . . Antichambrieren" . . . . "was raised to the level of a fineart by those sufficiently well connected and well dressed to secure entry. It was a subject of instruction at the Ritterakademien. *This was the golden age of adventurers. Casanova and Cagliostro were only the most famous of a host of plausible knights of fortune.*" Bruford, *Germany in the Eighteenth Century*, p. 104.

Extravagant and demoralizing courts were not a German monopoly. Some think that the sight of the wasteful and absurd court apparatus after Louis XVI moved from Versailles to Paris was one of the causes of the alienation of the people from the crown. After the Bourbon restoration, although the worst follies of the old order were now impossible, the lavishness of the court of Louis XVIII astonished Wellington as much as did the silliness of some of its members. And it is from this epoch that there dates that famous tirade of Paul Louis Courier against the whole race of courtiers. "L'offrande n'est jamais pour le saint, ni nos épargnes pour les rois mais pour cet essaim dévorant qui sans cesse bourdonne autour d'eux depuis leur berceau jusqu'à Saint-Denis."

court circle.[1] Had the Prussian monarchy been made an institution embodying unity and tradition while losing its active power, as in England, it might have survived and saved Germany and the world a great deal of trouble. But, of course, there was no point in having a constitutionally controlled monarchy without a constitutionally controlled army, press, bureaucracy, etc. The decline of the monarchy left a gap which only free institutions, freely accepted and worked in good faith, could have filled. The gap was filled by Hitler, who parodied William II even to the extreme length of going further to produce still more dreadful catastrophes for the German people—and their neighbours.

[1] It was quite useless playing at divine right and unbroken hereditary succession in a state like Bismarck's Prussia-Germany. The Kaiser was a newcomer in Bavaria and the Prussian King a recent usurper in Hanover. He behaved like the *parvenu* he was.

III

But as has been suggested, even if Bismarck had not succeeded in stifling what chances there were of turning the Prussian military monarchy into a free state, even if the transition had been made from the monarchy of William I to a monarchy representing the more liberal ideas of Frederick III and assuming that, on the throne, Frederick would have been content with a position like that of his mother-in-law, Queen Victoria, there would still have remained the great obstacle of the excessive place given in the Prussian and German tradition to the military aristocracy.

There is something formally attractive and plausible in the picture of a military aristocracy, imposing on itself a severe and almost monastic discipline, taking its reward austerely in honour, not political power or cash. Dreams of such a ruling caste were, it should be remembered, plausible enough to take in Plato. He admired the Spartan system of *paideia*, "a process by which the life of each citizen should be shaped to conform with some absolute norm."[1] They took in the less critical Plutarch. Faced with the degeneracy of Athenian democracy, the Athenians and those other Greeks who were bred in the Athenian spirit lavished on Sparta their literary talents, their philosophical talents, their myth-making talents. They had to do it, for Spartan education was too sterilizing to produce even effective myths. It did not even breed enough Spartans to make the military dominance of Sparta permanent; it did not breed enough political talent to make the political dominance of Sparta last more than a few years or have any permanent results. It did not even exempt the Spartans from human weakness, once outside of their artificial cage. The Spartan abroad was notorious for his corruption, his drunkenness, his greed. So too have been the Nazi officials in the occupied countries, who have added new disgrace to the German name by their combination of brutality and venality. In Bohemia they have

[1] *Werker Jaeger, Paideia*, p. 81 (English translation).

made the Czechs develop a new admiration for the comparative honesty and efficiency of Austrian days, as well as making them totally immune to *Herrenvolk* preaching in the present. In France they destroyed very rapidly the moral and political prestige won by the German victory of 1940. But the Prussian officer, the Prussian noble is not a "mere Nazi." No, but he has been an ally, a profiteer, an accomplice of the Nazis, all the same, and there would be substantial justice in a mere shrugging of the shoulders in a "tu l'as voulu, Georges Dandin" attitude on the part of the Allies or of the German masses alike.

That would be justifiable but not enough. For the case against the Prussian ruling class goes further back and is more fundamental. If he and his allies overthrew Brüning and opened the gates to Hitler because there was danger that the subsidies paid them as *Osthilfe* might be cut off, they were only acting in character. If the Prussian state collapsed with such ignominy in 1806 it was largely because the Prussian military nobles, for all their formal devotion to the dynasty, their indifference to political ambition in the English or American sense, did, in fact, sabotage the land reforms of Frederick the Great as they were to limit the land reforms of Stein. Their loyalty had very recognizable economic limits:

> "Und der König absolut
> Wenn er uns den Willen tut."

This class, the nearest approach to a political ruling class that Germany in modern times has produced, was not much better than the Polish nobility that sabotaged the reformers of eighteenth-century Poland. Refusing to accept political responsibility, it refused either to undertake or permit the necessary reforms that would have freed Germany from that *damnosa hereditas*, the political inheritance of the serf-economy of the trans-Elbian lands.

If we wish to see this failure in its historical context we must look at the success, at the conduct of a real civilian aristocracy, the English aristocracy. It is not a matter of moral superiority; the English aristocracy was selfish, corrupt and often stupid (so the American Revolution was made necessary). It did not always learn from experience, at any rate not quickly. It did not learn from the American Revolution the necessity of letting the remaining colonies move rapidly towards freedom. It thought it learned that the thirteen successfully revolted colonies had had too much freedom, so it made more efforts than ever before to control the remaining colonies of North America. Two generations passed before the mission of Lord Durham, sent to Canada to investigate the causes of the Canadian rebellion, began the modern process of making the British colonies independent nations, a policy whose prodigious success Britain has had cause to rejoice in and imperial and Nazi Germany alike, cause to lament. Even in 1840 there was no unanimous approval of this policy. The Duke of Wellington, a great, intelligent and critical soldier, but all the same a soldier, was full of the gloomiest prophecies. But the Duke's fears were not listened to; the great event that made the new colonial policy possible had occurred, the Great Reform Bill of 1832. Rare indeed in history are the cases when a ruling class manages to retreat in good order, to give way in time to the claims of a new class. No wonder the makers of the Reform Bill saw it as one of the great events of civilized history and saw its true parallel in the Licinian Rogations, in that concession of a share in the power of the Roman state made by the patricians to the plebs. Out of that ancient legal revolution came, so the English reformers thought, the most English of ancient states, the *Senatus Populusque Romanus*. So they thought, and rightly thought, would be restored the concord of the English people. "All history," said Macaulay in his most famous speech, "all history is full of revolutions, produced by causes similar to those now operating in England. A portion of the community which had been of no account expands and becomes strong. It demands a place in the system, suited, not to its former weakness, but to its present power. If this is granted all is well. If this is refused then comes the struggle between the young energy of one class and the ancient privileges of another. . . . Now, while the heart of England is still sound, now, while old feelings and old associations retain a power and a charm which may too soon pass away, now in this your accepted time, now in your day of salvation, take counsel, not of prejudice, not of party spirit, not of the ignominious pride of a fatal consistency, but of history, of reason, of the ages which are past, of the signs of this most portentous time." So spoke to a still aristocratic Assembly a rising bourgeois intellectual, nominee in Parliament of a great noble, descendant of that Shelburne who had seen stupidity, selfishness and incompetence disrupt the First British Empire. Some of the listeners, it is possible, remembered the words, more remembered the lesson of that passage in the Declaration of Independence which recalled how his still loyal American subjects had appealed to George III. "In every stage of these Oppressions We have Petitioned for Redress in the most humble terms; Our repeated Petitions have been answered only by repeated injury." But if few remembered Jefferson, many knew of Burke, telling the House of Commons to rise above legalism, to rise above the mere discussion of their rights. "I am not determining a point of law; I am restoring tranquillity." Restoring tranquillity, maintaining tranquillity, is the main business of the statesman, the test of the competence of a ruler, single or multiple. And a purely military state is always a poor creator or restorer of tranquillity, internally or externally. The military remedy is force; it *is* a remedy, but it is a remedy that tempts its user to use it too often and mere force, repeated and repeated, needs stronger and stronger doses till the revulsion comes. The soldier in the military state does not learn political prudence or political patience. He finds the reservations of his civilian colleagues unintelligible and has at the back of his mind the dangerous belief that, when the worst comes to the worst, he can always take over. A lieutenant and half a dozen men were enough to disperse the Reichstag, said the Junker. One man armed can control ten men in their shirts, says the English version. And once the idea is accepted that this kind of control is fruitful, that once you have asserted power that way, you can then go on to use that power as usefully, as safely, as profitably, even for yourself, as you can use political power based on an obedience not so nakedly coerced, the ruin of the state is at hand. For it is not often that the first use of the sword to cut a political knot is the last; untying the knot is troublesome and requires habits that an army does not often make second nature, as politics does.

That the problem of the relationship of the military power to the civil is basic to the solution of the general problem of the existence of the free state, was no new discovery. The Roman Republic, warlike, militarist, rigid in its insistence on the primacy of power in its exterior relations, was yet, in its prime, most vigilant in keeping the army outside the city. The sword must be borne against the enemies of the Republic, under the orders of magistrates who were, inside the city, eminently civilian officers. The dangers of militarism were commonplaces of the political writing of the Renascence. In that great, successful and, if you like, Germanic Republic, the Netherlands, the gratitude due to the House of Orange, genuine and deserved as it was, did not induce either the burgher aristocracy or even the mass of the people to accept without question the primacy of the soldier princes.[1]

And in thus keeping in the foreground the question of who shall control the state and the spirit in which the state is organized, the Dutch, the English, the Romans were wise. When the Roman Republic saw the rise to power of generals like Marius, Sulla and the rest with their private armies, the days of the Republic were numbered.

The advantages, even from a military point of view, in not submitting everything in the state to the test of military efficiency as decided by mere military technicians, are discussed further on. But whatever grim necessity may have forced on the infant state-power of Brandenburg-Prussia a military principle of growth, whatever accidents determined that the unity of Germany should be made on a Prussian

[1] Thus in the controversies over peace and war, over the size and cost of the army that marked the last years of the short life of the Stadtholder, William II, the anti-monarchical party stressed the implicit threat to free institutions in the claims of the army. "The English people, said one of these pamphlets, were able to prove that their King was a tyrant merely by pointing out that he raised an army before parliament followed his example." (G. J. Renier, *The Dutch Nation*, pp. 112–13.)

basis, it is a fact to be noted and its consequences allowed for. It is not a question of high moral, or intellectual or aesthetic indignation at the fact that the inner structure of modern Germany is the Prussian state and that the Prussian state is, historically, the outgrowth of the "Intendantur der Armee." It is a matter of noting the difference between such a state, and states that, like Athens and Rome, England and the United States, the Dutch Republic and the Swiss Confederation, grew around political ideas and political institutions, round law courts and parliaments, round independent corporations and rival religious organizations. In all of these successful states, war and arms played a part, but they were political successes above all. Their military power was a function of their political and social organization. And for Prussia? Well, it will be necessary to quote Mirabeau more than once, "not a state possessing an army but an army possessing a state."

In such a state free political life is impossible. But the converse is to be noted. In the free state effective military life is not impossible, it may be attained again and again, for, as I shall try to show later on, the military state does not always even get what it pays so high a price for. In the free state the soldiers will share in the common attitude of their fellows from whom they are not cut off by a totally different culture and set of standards. The Duke of Wellington tells us of the astonishment with which a captured French general heard the most junior officers in Wellington's camp freely criticizing the military conduct of the commander-in-chief. "With us, he said, no one ventured to touch upon political or military matters unless it were *à la louange de l'Empereur*. And if one officer was imprudent enough to say a word not tending *à la louange de l'Empereur*, there was immediately dead silence in the company —not a sound was heard—except from General Dorsenne, who breathed through his nose."[1]

How significant is that dead silence in which even great soldiers find their power of independent judgment atrophied, in which the supreme chief himself, even a Napoleon, loses all sense of reality and in which catastrophe, accelerated or

---

[1] Stanhope, *Conversations with the Duke of Wellington.*

delayed by conspiracy, is the only way out. The soldier chief in such a military society never learns the necessary political prudence that he will need if and when he assumes a political role. Roon and Moltke, it seems clear, never realized how inferior they were to Bismarck, but there was Bismarck. But when the Bismarcks are no longer there, when there is no institutional substitute for the Frederick or the Bismarck, the price has to be paid. Then Ludendorffs decide to defy the United States with no notion of its power; then junior officers sharpen their swords on the steps of the French Embassy in Berlin, exulting in a war that was to lead in a few weeks to the disaster of Jena; then, like new versions of the sorcerer's apprentice, generals learn, in a few disastrous months, what it is to have tried to use a Hitler as a tool, as a mere political convenience for the more serious business of war. But politics include war and more wars have been lost by soldiers turned politician than by politicians turned soldier.

IV

At a time when the other nations of the European world were becoming unified, when the rulers were being forced to consider the *political* problems presented by the rise of the modern, bureaucratic state, with its standing army and its more and more effective claim to sovereignty, the German people was broken up into three hundred sovereign units.[1] There is a dramatic contrast between the rise to supremacy in the English state of the "High Court of Parliament," or in France the long conflicts between the "sovereign courts," the Parliaments of Paris, Bordeaux, Strasbourg, Metz, etc., and the decline into comic futility of the Imperial Supreme Court at Wetzlar, now only remembered because of the true but almost incredible account of its futility given by Goethe in *Dichtung und Wahrheit*. There is an even more striking contrast between the term "lex terrae," the "Law of the Land," which, in Magna Carta, became so important in seventeenth-century England and, as "the supreme law of the land," became the clue to the rule of law and the role of the Supreme Court in America and the concession to the feudal princes of Germany of the title "domini terrae," the "Lords of the Land," by Frederick II, seventeen years after Magna Carta. The motives of the English barons were no more elevated than those of the German princes. But the English barons had been educated or bullied into wanting a share of the commonly held sovereign power; the German princes each wanted a piece that he could take away and enjoy by himself in a corner.

The result of this breaking-up of the sovereign power into little bits was to make impossible in Germany those fruitful contests *within* a united state which made the political life of the Western world. Despite all efforts, the rulers of France, the Netherlands, England, the Swiss Cantons, had to harmonize different groups, passions, interests, none of them strong enough to impose their will on *all* the other sections without taking into

---

[1] If free knights, etc., are counted, there were many more.

consideration their wishes and prejudices, pride and interests. In Germany this education in the political art of living on, at any rate, peaceful terms, with people with whom you did not agree, could not be learned. Everybody was agreed in a German state, great or small, to obey and, what was more difficult, to respect the Prince.

Germany, for example, had her full share of religious dissent, that dissent which, in other countries, was so fruitful in forcing toleration on unwilling rulers and still more unwilling sectaries. But no good political results came from the religious disunity of the German people. Each little sovereign state lived its own isolated and unified political life like a monad in the system of the great seventeenth-century German philosopher, Leibniz, with the Holy Roman Empire a remote and ineffectual political version of God. But the Holy Roman Empire, although it had to permit diversity in religious and political organization in such imperial bodies as the Reichstag, never learned or taught useful political habits since those imperial institutions were purely ceremonial.

Of course, no country in Europe in the seventeenth century really made a success of the problem of religious toleration combined with national unity, the problem presented by the break-up of medieval unity at the Reformation. But the character of the empirical solution arrived at had great importance for the future of these countries. No one will deny the importance of the Revocation of the Edict of Nantes in France or its English equivalent, the breach of the Treaty of Limerick in Ireland by the triumphant English. The Catholics of the southern part of the Dutch Republic were perhaps the least harassed of religious minorities, but their grievances, genuine as they were, left traces in Dutch history that only political sagacity and the necessities of toleration and co-operation imposed by democratic politics have made negligible in the present century. Uniformity enforced by persecution created modern Spain. And in Germany, a milder version of the same policy produced a peculiar German political and religious problem. For the application of the principle of *cujus regio, ejus religio*, the acceptance of the principle that the religion of the ruler should be the religion of the ruled, meant in the Germany of the three hundred odd independent rulers of the Peace of Westphalia, that there was a checker-board of religions, Catholic, Lutheran, Calvinist, but that *inside* each of these units there was uniformity. Since there was no common political life, there was no habit of common life overriding religious differences. Since there was an emigration of the minorities from states whose rulers persecuted them, there was no equivalent of the gain in political vigour by which France and England to some degree offset the loss of persecution. The minorities in England and France, in Holland and America, learned pride, tenacity, hostility to state pretension to infallibility. The German dissenter did not stay a dissenter, or he did not stay in the state in which he was a dissenter. It is to this fact, more than to any particular fondness for the right of the state to interfere in religion, that we owe the conformism of German church leaders. It is surely worth noting that the Catholic equivalent of Lutheran docility towards the Prince, "Josephism," was not effectually attacked until the peace settlement of Vienna had transferred a large area of the Catholic Rhineland to Protestant Prussia. Ferdinand Walter and Archbishop Droste-Vischering might not have found so much support for resistance to the power of the Prussian state if that state had been Catholic or even less aggressively Protestant. The Catholic workers who rallied to the Church's defence were in part moved by their dislike of their predominantly Protestant employers. We should not look the gift horse in the mouth; there was then, and later in the *Kulturkampf*, a genuine protest against state worship. If there had been large Lutheran communities harassed by Catholic rulers in, say, Bavaria, Lutherans too might have learned a distrust of the state that, politically, would have been of great value. Both Catholic and Protestant alike have since learned that putting your trust in princes or Führers is suicidal folly for Christian men, but it is late in the day and the habit of keeping the nation's conscience, against the nation's rulers, if needs be, is not deeply rooted yet in German churchmen or in their followers.

The failure to learn the difficult art of living with groups or

individuals with whom you are in disagreement, or even in
hereditary feud, had to be paid for in the nineteenth century.
For Germans still thought in the political patterns imposed by
their experience of little units of complete sovereignity. German
parties, at any rate the more important ones, thought of themselves as covering more of their members' lives than the mere
political aspects. It was a new application of *cujus regio, ejus
religio*, to make a party not merely a political organization,
but an organizer of culture, of youth movements, of music and
sport. In a free society of the Western type this temptation
suggests itself to political leaders, but against it there is the
habit of joining or not joining the churches, clubs, sports
associations that you prefer, whether they have an ideological
harmony with your party politics or not. Some correlations are
likely, but there are enough apparent contradictions to make
these independent organizations training-grounds for spontaneous, co-operative action, not necessarily hostile to the state
or the party, but not assimilated to either. The very emptiness
of the ideological content of American party programmes
ensures that, when groups and regions and individuals *are*
working together, there is something in it for them. They are
not obeying an automatic command or habit that bids them
co-operate, in a fixed way, with these people and not with
those. The member of an American party learns very little
about the bias of someone whom necessity forces him to work
with, by learning that he too is a member of the same party.
An Englishman meeting one type or class in his party, another
in his church, another in his football club, reading a very
unideological newspaper and, for a great part of the time,
more interested in his garden than in the affairs of the state, is
prepared to be interested and effectually interested in the
affairs of the state when they come home to his emotion and
judgment, an emotion and judgment fortified and trained by
many activities that are not, in the formal sense, political at all,
but which for that very reason have bred political habits. A
party in a free state has got to get used to the comparative
absence of undivided attention with which its slogans are
received. Of course, the party militants will largely consist of

people who believe that the one thing needful is the triumph of the party and of its programme. It is good that there should be many militants; it is also good that there should be many people who do not believe this, or only believe it at rare crises when it may well be true. The majority will in normal times be slightly bored, slightly sceptical, but its general support of a party is proof, not that it is at all times full of party zeal or party faith but that it accepts the need for political continuity, that it is willing to sacrifice something of its complete freedom of choice among measures and men, so that the machine of the free state may be kept ticking over, ready for the few occasions in which all this unorganized energy may be called on for national or even for party ends, in those crises in which some great national cause unites all, or when it has finally come to the point when a new direction of the state must be decided on. The inconsistencies of party, its reliance on mere habits, its imposing of impediment to the marriage of true minds, its creation of barriers between people who, for the moment, think alike concerning the commonwealth, all are to be admitted—and justified. They are the price to be paid for what party does, reduce the risks of atomizing political life and, for a temporary symmetry, making continuous free government impossible.

By training the voter in moderation, in philosophical acceptance of the limitations of government and yet giving him a real feeling that his consent is needed, is valuable and, in the mass, is decisive, the political party in the free state performs a most useful educational function. And because the coercive power of the party, as such, is small, the party leaders have to learn the difficult art of persuasion instead of falling back on the too easy remedy of coercion. There *is* a chain of command from top to bottom and each link has this healthy weakness, that the individual member can leave the party, join others or resume the important position of the independent voter whose vote or abstention is so often decisive. The independent voter, whether he knows it or not, sacrifices, as a rule, his chance of positive action, but his "no" is often decisive and usually, though not always, it represents the refusal of sensible men to believe nonsense or to throw good money after bad. The "Mugwump," as he is called in America, is the necessary complement of the good party man and he can only exist in a society in which the habit and duty of saying "no" have been encouraged by all kinds of institutions, not merely by political institutions.

The "Mugwump" fulfils another very important function. He ensures that the politician will watch with anxious care (sometimes, no doubt, too anxious care) those movements of opinion that can so easily turn into tidal waves of disapproval for hitherto invincible political leaders. It is not that the Member of Parliament or the Congressman is likely to revolt against the party leaders (it is much more likely in America than in England) as much as that he can tell his party leaders that such a course of action, if persisted in, will alienate the independent voter and may even drive off a few of the faithful. The politician thus talking to his chiefs has an interest in frankness that is rare indeed in the totalitarian state, where it is so much safer to tell the dictator only what he wants to know, since the only person whom you need please and whose anger is important is the dictator.

But the most popular and powerful democratic leader has a real motive for listening to the well-grounded fears of his lieutenants, since they stand or fall together if the people turns against them. So a healthy democratic society never gets into that condition common to dictatorships in which, until the very moment of catastrophe, there is a conspiracy of optimistic silence, of which dictator and people alike are victims. Block-leaders and spies snooping on a frightened people to report to illusion-fed chiefs are poor substitute for the brutal political truths told by second-rank politicians to first-rank politicians, both afraid of their sovereign master. There is a constant dosing of unpalatable truth that keeps the body politic healthy.

Of course, no party in a free state that insisted on complete, genuine ideological unity uniting its members and ignoring all other forms of unity, could last. Each party would then be a temporary coalition of people whose primary political aim was their sole bond of union, a bond that could not survive success. Thus special political organizations, like the Anti-Corn

Law League in England, practically dissolved with the attainment of their object. But the other problems of government were not suspended during the agitation for the abolition of corn laws nor did they cease with the abolition of the corn laws. A party is not a mere expression of a general principle; we are all against the man-eating shark. The problem of politics is *how* to deal with the man-eating shark or his equivalents. Nor is a party simply the vendor of a panacea. It is an instrument of government which has general principles (often so general as to be nearly meaningless); it has one or more projects which may be formally panaceas; but it is also, and this is the overriding purpose, an organization of government personnel.

It is because "splinter parties," formed to secure one reform, neglect the need for continuous administration, for the keeping before the voters alternative leaders (who need not be confined to two groups but cannot be unlimited in number), that they weaken the effectiveness of free government. For free government is a day-to-day habit, a continuous political training in mutual respect and collaboration, in maximizing consent and minimizing coercion; it is not, as some simple democratic apologists think, a mere matter of legislative or administrative edicts backed by majorities. The Republican leader in the United States who is reported to have said, "When the American people want socialism the Republican party will give it to them," was jesting, but there was wisdom in the jest. A party is an organized instrument of securing consent. In a fortunate community (such as the United States has been for a great part of its history) it is hard to say in advance "consent to what," but the parties play their great national role all the same. They are training-grounds, breeding-grounds for politicians, the only alternative governing class to courtiers, policemen, soldiers, gangsters.

V

In those lesser societies that, without being rivals to the party or the state, do at least limit their political monopoly, is to be found one of the secrets of the health of the free state. The citizen is insulated against the exclusive claims of the controller of state authority without being in any inevitable danger of being made indifferent to the legitimate authority of the state, an authority that is based on so many different forms of consent and co-operation. Sometimes it will be necessary to make a final decision; and that decision will not be popular with all, but it will be the more willingly accepted that it is the decision of a state that is accustomed to win consent when it can.

And that consent, whether it is emotional or intellectual, is won in *competition*. It would be absurd to pretend that Hitler has not often won consent and that the totalitarian state has no effective means of winning consent. Indeed, being monopolistic, the totalitarian state can, by excluding critical voices and making dissent dangerous, by complete control of education, the press, the radio, the cinema, secure a kind of consent that is, emotionally if not morally, highly useful to the rulers of the state. But it will be used by them in proportion to their own wisdom and moral integrity which we have no reason to believe will remain high. The consent won in the free state is harder won and harder-wearing. Nevertheless, it does not last; it has to be renewed again and again and the necessity for getting that consent renewed is chastening for the rulers—and good for them.

It is easy to point out the grave imperfections of free speech and the free press in a free society. What is the use of an abstract right to start a newspaper if only a millionaire can do it? What is the use of free speech if the publicity necessary to get you an audience needs a millionaire's resources or a great and, consequently, established organization? If government or commercial authorities control all the good radio time what is the meaning of free speech on the air? Questions of this type could

be put for page after page. But it is to be observed, in the first
place, that these criticisms are often covers for despair. It is too
hasty a retreat from the problem of the free press to fall back
on a monopolistic press, to point to the worst sins of the capita-
list press as a justification for falling into the depths represented
by the *Völkischer Beobachter* or the Mannheim *Hakenkreuz
Banner*. Even Bismarck's reptile press was better than that. And
why? Because not only were there non-reptile journals, but
there were many more instruments of influencing public
opinion, the Reichstag and Landtags of the states, trade
unions, parties, churches, most of them harassed and timid by
Western standards, but nevertheless obstacles to a complete
unification of German public opinion based on a monopoly of
opinion-forming resources.

The problem of free discussion and consent in the new conditions of free society, conditions in which it is certain that the
share of the state in economic control will necessarily increase
and in which the scale of most communal undertakings will
increase, is a very real one. But it is not insoluble if will is
devoted to solving it and despair (disguised as rigid moral and
intellectual standards) is not made an excuse for passivity. In
Germany the question will be less that of salvaging an old and
deep-rooted tradition of free discussion and critical political
controversy, than of creating a habit of mind in which criticism
is accepted, even if it is not very responsible or well-informed.
It is not very long since the trials for *lèse-majesté* were a
feature of the Second Reich and trials for unpatriotic candour
in criticizing secret rearming were not unknown under the
Weimar régime. The concept of free discussion, even of matters
of state and even by amateurs, is not old in Germany.
John Peter Zenger was able to defend the freedom of the press
successfully in 1735, but that was because he had emigrated to
New York instead of staying in his native Germany.

For another of the unfortunate results of the division of
Germany was the postponement of the question of the political
commentator in the free state. In the divided Germany of the
eighteenth century, there could not be a real national opinion.
But in some states it was possible to set up as critic of the poli-

tical life—of other states. Thus A. L. von Schlözer, in Hanover, could exercise a good deal of influence, the more that Hanover, through its dynastic connection with England, had more generous conceptions of political life than had most other German states. But Schlözer could not have criticized the Elector George III as Wilkes criticized King George III, or rather, there was no chance at all of making Schlözer a martyr to the freedom of the press as Wilkes became, to his considerable profit. In a state like Württemberg, Julius Moser could, thanks to the slightly more liberal political institutions, reach the rank of martyr. But he could not make a career of it.

When we think of the great names of Western literary-political tradition, Milton, Voltaire, Swift, Montesquieu, Rousseau, Franklin, Jefferson, Hamilton, Madison, Burke, and try to find German names of equal weight, we are on the trail of one of the problems not faced in Germany, the provision of critical, unofficial comment on government action. In a culture with names like these among its greatest, there was no danger of the educated classes becoming unduly credulous or accepting, in the fashion of too well disciplined children, the dogma that "papa knows best." Since these men of great eminence and weight often opposed not only the official but the unofficial opposition story too, there was less danger of belief in the secret wisdom of authority or of counter-authority.

It is again an unfortunate part of the German historical inheritance that there is an inadequate tradition of the study of the working of a free society, even of the mere mechanical devices of a free society. What could the small German states provide in the way of opportunity or freedom for such a study? Some of the officials, or the professors or the paid controversialists of the German states, were men of talent, many were men of learning, some were men of political judgment and virtue. But what impression is made, even on a German by a list of the disciples of Pufendorf? Do we or they care if his theories were adopted by "Thomasius, Titius, Gundling . . . both the Cocceji, Stryck, Ickstatt, Kreittmayr, Heincke"?[1]

---

[1] *Natural Law and the Theory of Society 1500 to 1800*, by Otto v. Gierke translated, with an introduction, by Ernest Barker, vol. I, p. 144.

What are such names compared with men who had the good fortune to live in real political societies, Grotius, Milton, Locke, Montesquieu, Rousseau, Jefferson, Burke, Madison, or the German Althusius with the Dutch Republic close at hand to feed his mind and spirit? What kind of political education did Goethe get in the petrified patrician republic of Frankfort compared with that given to Jakob Burckhardt in the patrician families of Basel?

The cameralist making a case for his Prince, or rationalizing the mere administration, is a poor figure beside Jefferson or Burke. And it was not merely an accident, it is a result of an institutional bias and a planned bias, that the German people, on the eve of their first great modern crisis, were so ill prepared for it.

Writing in 1907, the great Austrian jurist, Joseph Redlich, noted this :

"Nowhere has the tendency to belittle parliaments been more marked than in countries where the German conception of the state has been adopted, both within and without the bounds of the present German Empire. This is, of course, in the main, a consequence of certain great historical events; in no other area has parliamentary government found such difficulty in taking root or entered so little into the popular idea of the state. One result of German mistrust, in my opinion, has been that in no single department of the theory of the modern state has German research been so unfruitful as in that of parliamentary government. However instructive it might be to speak the whole truth as to some recent theories on the subject, I do not propose here to say a word about them. But quite apart from this, how little, for example, has been attempted in the way of historical investigation into German parliamentary systems, what a gap would be filled by a history of political parties in Germany and their influence upon the development of representative institutions!

"An investigation of the reasons why so little has been done would lead us too far. I only mention it for the purpose of pointing out that there is here a most important task for German political philosophy still to perform, one the accomplishment of which is a veritable state necessity."[1] It *was* a state necessity, but a necessity for which the rulers of the anti-parliamentary state of Prussia-Germany naturally gave no priorities. And a tradition of academic freedom that was far from encouraging forms of *Lernfreiheit* which might have awkward results for the state that made, paid and controlled the universities, was not likely to lead to the production of studies of problems which the state's rulers thought were no problems at all. It was all right to have "socialists of the chair" advocating the extension of the power of the state, but what if they went on to discuss who should control the reinforced state? They did not. And no number of academic exponents of the beauties of state action in the economic field were an adequate substitute for continual criticism of state action in all fields—and amateur criticism at that. Whether Virchow was a useful scientific member of the Reichstag is less important than whether he was a useful member of the Reichstag in fields in which he had no special competence.

Academic freedom has not been totally observed in England, and still less in America, but at any rate the ideal of free research, free discussion, even in fields that no one else thinks important, and free discussion before non-academic audiences, is deeply rooted and, if not a perfect barrier to the intrusion of political control from above or business control from outside, is yet a barrier. And more important still, there is no tradition at all that all important political thinking is the work of professors or other state officials. A man may be an outcast professor like Veblen, in America, or not a professor at all like John A. Hobson, in England, or be by professorial calling a chemist and by choice a theorist on money; it is his right, not as a professor but as a citizen, to have views, to get them expressed as best he can and to convert his fellow citizens, learned and unlearned, not merely to assent but to action. A professor who is a socialist in his chair but never from a soapbox is merely a more sophisticated form of an idiot.

For there is no such thing as political or economic science in

[1] Joseph Redlich, *The Procedure of the House of Commons: A Study of its History and Present Form* (English translation), vol I, pp. xxvi–xxvii.

the sense of a number of recipes for ills and preventives of evil. What we shall think remedies depends on what what we think are diseases; and all political and economic remedies have their price and whether we think that price high or low, dear or cheap, depends on our total view of what we really prize. And in a free society, too, the remedy adopted depends on whose views of the remedy and its price are listened to. The free state tries to ensure that everybody who has views can speak them; it tries to create a public attitude which does not rule out, in advance, views coming from obscure men or unpopular groups. In all these attempts it fails; its success can never be complete but any success in this attempt is better than the organized opposition to such inadequate attempts to provide institutional bases for the right of the individual, poor, silly, rich, silly, to have his say, his own opinions, to contribute a tiny drop to the great ocean of national life. The basic success is attained when the private citizen feels that he is not totally debarred from free speech, free action, a share in the sovereignty, when he feels that the state in which he lives is not one in which he has no duty but obedience, no means of judgment but those given him by his rulers at their good pleasure. Democracy begins at this point; it does not end there and, indeed, never ends, is never fully attained. But it is a beginning when it is accepted as "the palpable truth, that the mass of mankind has not been born with saddles on their backs, nor a favoured few booted and spurred, ready to ride them legitimately, by the grace of God." The notion of legitimacy has changed since Jefferson's day; it is now a legitimacy of race, of political inspiration, of political orthodoxy once for all delivered to the founders of parties become the rulers of states. But the free peoples still resist the saddle and see in the boots and spurs no proof of rightness, no proof of permanence, no substitute for the power that comes from persuasion, for the leadership that can admit it may have been wrong, that is not bound to a disastrous infallibility and omniscience against which the whole human race is in unconscious conspiracy.

Again, it is historical bad luck that the German people find this almost automatic reaction of the Western peoples so hard to feel. It is historically explicable that they feel the burdens of self-rule more than they feel the charm of it. And it is historically unfortunate that the elements of free organization that were present, in the German Middle Ages as elsewhere, only got a chance to develop in the outlying parts of the old German Empire, in the Netherlands, in Switzerland, and in those free cities which, like Hamburg, were always kept in touch with the greater world by trade. Of course, in large Hansa towns like Frankfort, there was a better education in the politics of persuasion than was possible in the large principalities, much more the small principalities. But the Hansa towns did not play a real role in general German politics and the few states that had a rudimentary political life like Württemberg were not powerful enough to change the general tone of German society.

Thus the German aristocracy never developed the necessary political habits of a real aristocracy. In England a great noble-man like the Duke of Bedford was far richer than most German princes, but he had no serious political power that he owned independently of his ability, personality, industry. Of course, as a wealthy duke, he had means of persuading the voters that a poor man did not have, but he had to persuade them. And in the course of that persuasion he was continually reminded that, great magnate as he was, his power, his wealth, his dignity, were the fruits of a general political system that guaranteed the rights of very poor and weak people too. It did not guarantee very much, but that the poorest man in England had certain legal rights, that the traces of serfdom and serf status had vanished from law and custom, was very important. It was an old joke to laugh at the poor English sailor, seized by the press gang for the Navy, yet rejoicing in his superiority over Frenchmen and Germans as a beneficiary of English free-dom. That freedom was often of very little practical value indeed, but it was of great moral value. And a modern psycho-logist might hold that the conviction of a fixed, unalienable legal status treasured by the poor Englishman was not an unprofitable illusion, for it saved him from many interior conflicts, it gave him a place in the nation and in society of which he could not be deprived. It lessened temptations both to jealousy and resentment and helped to create that imperturbable self-esteem that Goethe liked in the young English noblemen he saw making the grand tour and that, in the darkest hours of 1940, was a barrier in rich and poor alike against which Nazi arms and Nazi propaganda stormed in vain.

In the United States the English situation was repeated in a more advanced form. There were no magnates on the scale of the Duke of Bedford; there was far more need for persuasion; there was a more general acceptance of the common legal rights of Englishmen, then of Americans. George Washington was the richest Virginian of his day, but that was not why he was the greatest Virginian of his day. He was, as President, both the great and respected national chief and hero, and willy-nilly, a political leader regarded with grave suspicion by zealous democratic leaders like Senator Maclay. When one thinks of the adulation poured out on a mediocrity like Hindenburg and the savage scrutiny of all the actions of President Washington that marked the early formative years of the American Republic, it is hard not to think that democratic vigilance has sometimes a high price in bad manners and ingratitude, high but not too high. The Virginian gentlemen of the eighteenth century produced Washington, Jefferson, Madison, Chief Justice Marshall. Two generations later Virginia only produced great soldiers, Lee, Jackson, Johnston; it was a change for the worse and it reflected the poisoning of Virginian life by the slavery question.

For we must not burke the ugly side of American democratic practice, negro slavery, racial discrimination after emancipation, lynching and mob violence. But we should remember how, usually silently but at times openly, the democratic principles and battle-cries have warred against slavery and its results, how it became harder and harder for slave-owners to repeat the great words of the Declaration of Independence asserting the right of all men to "life, liberty and the pursuit of happiness." The words stuck in the throat till the great anomaly was extinguished in blood. And so with modern milder variants. Great words, great names, great traditions slowly defeat the order based on racial inequality. Nazi Germany and pre-Nazi Germany, alas, have no such heritage of general principle that in the long run conquered stronghold after stronghold of the old, evil order.

Indeed, to many Germans, the "pursuit of happiness" has seemed an ignoble ideal, incapable of tragic splendour and revelatory of the material, unideal Western mind. Of course, the type of happiness pursued makes a great difference and the type aimed at may be very pedestrian or worse. But it also may be high as it was in the long life of the author of the phrase (Thomas Jefferson) and as it has been in many makers of Western civilization. That civilization has not forgotten its roots in Hebraic conceptions of duty and righteousness or its roots in Hellenic conceptions of the beauty of good action. Neither tradition is welcoming to mere harshness, mere love of destruction, mere barbarous asceticism such as has been taught, with more or less success, to young Germany in this century. There was no ignoble ease on the Virginia frontier where Jefferson grew up, and mere money-grubbers, mere utilitarians do not man air forces or armies like those that battered the Nazi fortress in France to pieces in a few weeks. But it should be admitted that the Western world *does* treasure happiness and amiability and ease of intercourse and avoidance of excessive and sterilizing use of force. The tone of its society in the home, in the school, even in the army, is not stiff, solemn, hierarchical, coercive. Even war is a way, a wasteful way, forced on them of keeping the pursuit of happiness as a practicable ideal. War is fought that toleration, ease, respect for human personality and even human oddity and unpredictability may be more and more the tone of Western society. That is what its politics are about.

Long disunited, the German people has paid a very high price for its political unity. It has, by hundreds of years of its history, been cut off from the Western experience in which the unity of the state has been taken for granted and that unity has been a unity in diversity. The accidents of the political unification of Germany have made military methods of securing

united action become political second nature to German statesmen—and they are poor methods of securing unity. A military
state will stress force more than is good, will underestimate
women, impose too rigid discipline on children, will shrink
from solutions that seem untidy to the military mind. It is true
that an army cannot afford the flexibility and rationality of a
civil state. There is justice in the criticism of a totally rational
army; "it would run away." But that is a reason for not making
the military way of doing things the normal way, even in the
army.

A free society is one that accepts risks of diversity, partly on
pragmatic grounds, partly because of a kind of mystical respect
for the unpredictable character of human action and the unpredictable problems posed by this very imperfectly mastered
world. It welcomes diversity even at the certainty of friction
and when unanimity comes (as at great moments it does),
thinks it all the more valuable for having come a long way
round, up and not down.

It would be idle to pretend that the diversity revealed by the
democratic process is always of a highly interesting kind. It
may be based on narrow conflicts of interest, on narrow prejudices of party and of persons, on nothing more edifying than
the human propensity, not discouraged in free societies, to
disagree from a kind of sporting instinct. It may be that there
are times in which only one policy could possibly appeal to a
disinterested and well-informed citizen and that nothing
prevents the unanimous acceptance of that policy but party
spirit and the habits it breeds. It may be that the opposition to
a policy is based on no more a dignified principle than that
"the duty of an Opposition is to oppose." And in these circumstances the supporters of the one wise policy, the administrators
who have to carry it out and who know that their opponents,
were they the government, would have to carry it out too,
may be pardoned if they get irritated by what may seem to be
the lack of scruple of the practising politician and the lack of
sense of the party voter. But there is a long-term interest in the
preservation of a critical public opinion that is more important
than the smooth and easy passage of even the most uncontest-

ably beneficial measure. The irritation the administrator or publicist or theorist feels at public pig-headedness is part of the price to be paid for the education of rulers in the necessary democratic art of persuasion.

For the free society believes that the quality of assent matters as well as the fact of assent. If after a long and bitter debate there is either a real conversion of the opposition or at any rate that kind of consent that comes from having had the chance to state the grounds of doubt and opposition, the policy thus put into effect has a better chance of political success than if it had been briefly and dogmatically made law by the fiat of the most enlightened ruler. Of course, the dream of a philosopher king or of a king who takes the advice of the philosopher appeals to the intellectual snob. It appeals to great men like Plato; it appeals to the apologists and worshippers of any authoritarian system. But few kings or princes or tyrants are notably enlightened. From Plato to Turgot, the role of the wise man using the political power of the absolute ruler to do good has been disappointing, to them and to the people concerned. Not only is the ruler's attention easily distracted, his selfish interest often quickly arrayed against the philosophical minister, but few effective pieces of legislation really work well if they are hastily imposed on a society that is not ready for them. They may produce dramatic results, the intoxication of the power to order great masses of human beings for their own good may for a time make the executants of the policy "drunk with success," but after the drunkenness there is the hangover.

And, in a great crisis, the unity of the free states is not inferior to the unity of the authoritarian states. It wears better; it is less associated with mere immediate success; it represents something personal to the citizen; it can be maintained by less hysterical means, by less diversion of the resources of the society to coercion and the forcible injection of right attitudes. It is very hard to get a docile and uncritical people and get also a ruling class that keeps its head. Free consent is, practically speaking, a method with a lot to be said for it. And even if it has no more to be said for it in pragmatic terms than has the coerced or induced consent of the totalitarian societies, there is a moral bias in the West in favour of it. That bias is old, it will be hard to root out. It has been stated in extravagant terms as if a majority is always right and, once the existence of a majority is established, there is no more to be said. It is sometimes associated with a contempt for the truth that not all questions are open questions; that some have been decided, once for all, and that there are fields in which expert opinion is conclusive, although the field in which there is, in social science, unanimity of expert opinion, is not very wide. But in the West we have for long believed that the assent of a slave or serf and the consent of a free man are different moral and political conceptions and that much else that we value for practical reasons is bound up with this moral and ideal preference.[1]

At the end of the last war, G. K. Chesterton commented thus on a famous war slogan: "The world will never be made safe for democracy, it is a dangerous trade." That was true and worth saying in those optimistic days. But better worth saying to-day is that free government is one of the greatest of the arts and one of the most rewarding, that a society which practises that art successfully is, for that alone, a great society and the exemplification of a high culture. (Almost always the free society can easily afford to stand comparison in other fields of culture too.) But the free life of a free polity has its own rules; it is not to be judged simply in terms of other arts, or by the standards and aesthetic preferences of philosophers or painters or would-be philosophers or painters. It is all right for the philosopher to ponder on the deepest problems of life, but life for the mass of men (including the philosophers and the artists) has to be lived. We must insist on the life of action and on its

[1] "We can truly say that *one* of the major respects in which a political order is to be regarded as a high moral and spiritual achievement is the respect in which it conforms to this ideal of a *societas* of freemanly wills, in other words, that the more a political order resembles the order in which knowledgeable men with a wide range of choice would freely accept and in which they would actively collaborate if they had the power, the better, *ceteris paribus*, such a political order would be. As it seems to me, we should not say more than this." (John Laird, *The Device of Government*, p. 71.) But a German would need to be warned against translating "knowledgeable men" into "experts."

rights and rules. We must accept the politician as well as the pure thinker, Pericles as well as Plato. We must accept the implications of the words of a great living philosopher who is in no danger of underestimating Plato: "Plato's own writings constitute one prolonged apology for freedom of contemplation, and for freedom for the communication of contemplative experiences. In the persistent exercise of this right Socrates and Plato lived, and it was on its behalf that Socrates died. There are exceptional passages, but throughout the bulk of the Dialogues Socrates and Plato are engaged in expressing manners of thought. Hardly ever is there a passage which can be directly translated into a particular action. The conclusions of the Republic will work only in heaven. . . . The Thucydidean Pericles stresses the other side. He is thinking of the activities of the individual citizens. The peculiar civilization of the speech arises from its stress upon the aesthetic end of all action. A barbarian speaks in terms of power. He dreams of the superman with the mailed fist. He may plaster his fist with sentimental morality of Carlyle's type. But ultimately his final good is conceived as one will imposing itself upon other wills. This is intellectual barbarism. *The Periclean ideal is action weaving itself into a texture of persuasive beauty analogous to the splendour of nature.*"[1]

The day-to-day mechanics of free politics may not reach this height very often. There will be Cleon as well as Pericles. The Athenian democracy slowly decayed. But even from the material point of view, Athens succeeded better than Sparta and the memory of one is cherished for itself while the other is mainly known by what its rival's sons have said of it. Athens, at least, did not sacrifice to mere existence the best reasons for existence and so as a memory and as a city it is still with us, while the site of Sparta is a village and Spartan life a faint memory. If we rejoice in the victory of Greece over Persia it is because the Athenians were Greeks, not because the Spartans were. And so it is to-day. Even in disaster the free state has made the better choice; its very enemies may lament it while the death of Assyria or the defeat of Prussia is final. The

[1] A. N. Whitehead, *Adventures of Ideas*, pp. 64–5. (Italics mine.)

democratic ideal is difficult of attainment, it looks both harder and, at times, less impressive than the mere ideal of power and discipline as ends in themselves. But life is on its side and so is the whole Western tradition of which Germany is a part.

CHAPTER THREE

LIBERTY AND ARMS

I

THE character of a state or society is often shown in small, significant things. And there is a deep meaning in the custom which ordains that a President of the United States, who is, by virtue of his office, Commander-in-Chief of the American Army and Navy, should never wear military uniform, even though he has been a soldier in the past. Many Presidents have been soldiers; three of them, Washington, Jackson, Grant, were great, victorious soldiers, but it was not as soldiers but as civil officers that they were Commanders-in-Chief. The contrast with Germany is striking. William II was not only hereditary war lord, but he so exulted in the office that while his uniforms were carefully made, his civilian tailor had to guess from the shape of the uniforms what kind of civilian clothes would fit. It was beneath the dignity of the Kaiser to be measured for civilian clothes. As a civil officer, any ready-to-wear garment was adequate. In the same way, that eminently civilian official, the Chancellor, Bethmann-Hollweg, always addressed the old imperial Reichstag in uniform; that civilian of genius, Bismarck, on all great occasions wore the uniform of a colonel of cuirassiers, and even under the Weimar Republic, the defeated general, Hindenburg, very often wore, as President of the Republic, the uniform of his army rank—which, as has been said, no American victorious soldier-President ever did.[1]

[1] In England, only one soldier has ever become Prime Minister, the Duke of Wellington. Even on the battlefield, the Duke wore a kind of semi-civil dress and his most famous lieutenant, Sir Thomas Picton, commanded in a tall hat. It was this indifference to the tailoring side of war that gives special point to the most famous story about Wellington. Leaving the palace after a levée in full field-marshal's uniform, he was accosted by a civilian who said, "Mr. Smith, I believe?" "If you believe that you will believe anything." Military men in full regalia were not as common in London as in Berlin.

It was not a minor matter, this difference between the United States and the Second Reich, any more than it is a minor matter that the Third Reich has put all public officers into uniform, has imposed universal salutes and greetings and has made the difference between civil and military life, between the barracks and the home, or school, or factory, so slight, and before war had been openly made, had already imposed so many of its burdens on the German people. Hitler announcing in 1939 that he would never take off his uniform-coat till victory was won is a very different leader from Mr. Churchill, changing from one type of uniform to another as his sense of comfort, fitness or humour suggests, and conducting a war to a victorious conclusion in a siren suit of civilian character and individual design. Even when a leader of a free society enjoys dressing-up, his choice is so personal that the word uniform is out of place and when he does wear uniform, he, like General Grant, may look less military at the head of a great army than Hindenburg did in a frock-coat addressing the Reichstag of republican Germany. Field-Marshal Montgomery, in his beret, slacks and umbrella, is a soldierly figure, but one in a very different tradition from that represented by Goering or Ludendorff.

What useful political truth is illustrated by this matter of dress? The useful truth that there is a difference between a civil state, a form of government in which war is a regrettable and rare activity of the community, and one in which the state and nation are in a perpetual state of preparation for or recovery from war. In one, war is the last argument; in the other, it is almost or quite the only argument—for it does not in this case matter very much whether *all* disputes are settled by arms or some by the mere threat of arms. A military, unpolitical state is one in which all institutions take their colour, their ways of working, the r public importance from the army whose pre-eminence is never in any dispute. Such a state was Prussia; such a state was the Second Reich; such a state was the Third Reich. "Prussia," said Mirabeau, "is not a state possessing an army but an army possessing a state." Prussia is not the only example. Ancient Sparta was another; Paraguay was another; the Zulu kingdom of Chaka was another. Such was not Rome; such are not Britain or the United States. And yet Rome, Britain, the United States, suffer not at all in comparison with Sparta or Prussia or the Zulus in any comparison of military achievement, or in any stocktaking of the results of a form of society and government conceived in terms of force and war and the results of a form of society in which politics, the supremacy of the civil magistrate, the domination of the law limit the power of the soldier. The military state wins victories but not campaigns, campaigns but not wars, for the simple reason that life is far more complicated than war and war far more than a mere business of soldiering. "War," said Clemenceau, "is far too serious a matter to leave to soldiers." It is—and a society that leaves it to soldiers, not only suffers from it in war but suffers from it in peace; in order to secure what victory can bring, it sacrifices so much that makes victory worth having—and, in the long run, does not get victory.

The civilian leaders of a civil state, when it is at war, will often make grave mistakes; the technical details of war cannot be as familiar to them as they are to a professional soldier. They will often listen to the wrong experts; they will often underestimate the professional who is incapable of ready speech and overestimate the brilliant talker and writer. Yet the experience of history suggests that these are not fatal defects. They are compensated for by qualities bred by civilian experience. As war has become more and more total, as it has involved the whole population, men, women, and children, it has become more and more political. The problem of organization is only, *up to a point*, a question of coercion. No coercion can compensate for complete exhaustion, no coercion can draw on resources that are not really there; above all, coercion, as such, can impose on the enemy material surrender when all hope is gone, but it cannot win him to acquiescence and the object of war is to disarm the *will* of the enemy. The habit of seeing all problems in the terms of orders given and taken, of relying, as any army must, on automatic if intelligent obedience, becomes a handicap as the war lasts, as new and unforeseen situations arise (as they must in any long war), as soon as the simple solution of a military victory quickly won is seen to be illusory. Then subtler qualities of mind and spirit are called for, then political talents are more important than merely military talents, then the country that has reserves of loyalty and independent, *private* spiritual resources wins the last round.

But it will be usually found that they have also won the real first round, the first round that is fought before the war begins. For the foreign policy, the diplomacy of a power whose basic character is military, will reflect the strength and weakness of the military mind and the military method. And it will reflect the weakness more than the strength. For within its own military sphere, military efficiency is real; outside it, military efficiency is inefficiency. It is no accident that Germany has twice managed to mobilize against herself overwhelmingly powerful coalitions of very reluctant enemies. Germany has been twice encircled—by herself. And the encirclement has been produced by the same methods that produced the early victories. It is of no avail to lament the sterility of those victories, to speculate that if this had happened one way, or that another, there would have been a breathing spell in which to enjoy or consolidate the fruits of victory. The victories were gained by the sacrifice, in peace, of those civilian qualities of compromise, legality, caution, which, of course, make preparation for aggressive war difficult and, indeed, impossible. But that they do make aggressive war difficult and in most cases impossible, is evident to the rest of the world as well. So, too, is the fact that the sacrifice of everything that, in peace-time, stands in the way of preparation for war, makes aggressive war tempting, easy and, in a sense, habitual. The very politicians and diplomats of the military state will fall easily into military manners, will threaten instead of negotiating, will bully instead of persuading. They *will* succeed in frightening their neighbours, at first into concessions, but then into resistance. It is not only German history that illustrates this point. It was King Louis XIV who put on his cannon the threatening Latin motto, "ultima ratio regum," the "last argument of kings." And intoxicated by success, increasingly careless of the public opinion of Europe—or of France—Louis XIV began to make it the first argument too. And so, despite a union of cultural and military prestige that Germany has never known, despite an intrinsic predominance that no other country has ever had, despite great soldiers and sailors and diplomatists, the France of Louis XIV forced Europe to combine to end this nightmare. The Dutch were forced to make a revolution to resist him; the English were forced to abandon a profitable neutrality; even the Hohenzollerns were forced to pay some regard to the general interests of Germany and Europe. The overweening power of France was curbed and, on his deathbed, Louis XIV repented of his political sin of loving war too much. No doubt he repented sincerely but his repentance was undoubtedly stimulated by the fact that the Duke of Marlborough and Prince Eugene (a native of Paris) turned the King's arguments against him—as Swift said when he heard of the great captures of French guns at Blenheim.

Napoleon repeated the lesson; he too drove his enemies together, forced even Prussia to take up arms with the odds against her, made all peace treaties mere truces and, sacrificing all independence of thought and action in France to making war, found that the greatest of all soldiers could not win. He, less wise than Louis XIV, never fully understood the causes of his defeat but they were plain enough. He would not let the rulers of Europe or the peoples of Europe alone. The temptation to exploit his military supremacy overcame him again and again until the continent realized that there would be no peace with Napoleon, that you could not do business with him any more than you could do business with Hitler.

Yet the rulers of France had great advantages that Germany has not. European culture in the age of Louis XIV and Napoleon was still predominantly French. Modern democracy was either not born or a weak infant, the peoples of Europe often counted for little enough in the decisions of their rulers. The French conquests were far less resented than any foreign conquests could be to-day. Even so, European society was too conscious of its own rights, of its own pride and duty, to submit. The sections of European society that looked with a friendly eye on French power, the Republican party in seventeenth-century Holland, Beethoven or Charles Fox in the age of the French Revolution, were driven into hostility and resistance.

There never has been, in this sense, a German cultural predominance in modern Europe. Too much, far too much, was sacrificed to secure material predominance for the spectacle of the power of the Second Reich to evoke more than respect. No Frenchman or Englishman looked on the work of Bismarck with the sympathetic understanding that Goethe gave to the work of Napoleon. But Bismarck knew (as Frederick the Great learned) that too open a defiance of the interests of the other European states, too complete moral and material isolation, was fatal. To prevent that isolation, to give an appearance of moderation, Bismarck was ready to cheat, to lie, to forge. But he had the supreme political virtue of knowing when to stop, when to cease to threaten. He knew that he could not make Germany strong enough to fight all Europe—and so he took care not to force all Europe to fight Germany. He made concessions to defeated France, he refused to exploit to the full his victory over Austria. He fought only partially successful battles with the soldiers who never understood how much they owed to the man who secured for them the limited wars in which their mere technical supremacy could be exploited. What they, the Prussian experts in recipes for victory, lost when they lost Bismarck, 1914 and 1939 were to show. War in 1914, like war in 1939, was a confession of political *incompetence* by the rulers of Germany, blinded by their habits of mind, bred in corporal and general alike, by the neglect of the civilian and political truths that can only be learned in a militaristic state by a genius like Bismarck and yet, in a civil state, in a real political organization, are taught by the whole structure of society to quite mediocre politicians. And, what is more important, they are daily learned by the free peoples on whom these mediocre politicians can draw for more than bravery and obedience, for originality, for ideas, for the moral resources to stand a long war and the untired, unplanned versatility that wins long wars. The military state can only plan for and win short wars and, planning for short wars, it almost always behaves in a fashion to secure that the war will not be short and so will be lost. If the object of military efficiency is to win wars, military efficiency, in the German sense, is a contradiction in terms.

For the apparent paradox is yet the truth. Real total war is more easily attained by a free state than by a purely military state.

The reasons for the apparent paradox are not very hard to find. Both the military state and the free state, in modern war, will be called on to use all their resources. The military state can, in peace-time, call on far more of the available resources than can the free state. No people readily prefers guns to butter. It has to be conditioned by propaganda, by doses of political dope, by the simple refusal of any free choice, to accept the imposition, in time of formal peace, of the basic conditions of open war, the concentration of all the economic power of the state on providing the materials of modern war. A free people like the English, even when danger is imminent, will prepare less thoroughly than the Third Reich prepared for the dangers created by its rulers. (After all, the rulers of England and the English people could have illusions about the character and designs of the rulers of the Third Reich that those gentlemen could not have about themselves.) A free state can prepare, more or less efficiently, more or less thoroughly. But, at the best, it will still be spending on butter some resources that the military state bent on war will spend on guns. It will still have shadow war factories while the military state has real war factories. The story current in Berlin round 1936 makes the point. The worker in a baby carriage factory decided to steal each day one part of the baby carriage, naturally, since his wife was expecting a baby and the German worker, even as early as that, had no spare resources; it was not only butter that was given up! After a time he had accumulated all the necessary parts but, as he said to his wife, "no matter what I do, it always turns out to be a machine-gun."

In the free state, no matter what the rulers do, some people will insist, in peace-time, when the danger is not over-

whelmingly evident, on baby carriages and butter. Free from
the need of paying attention to such people, the army state can
go ahead. It can mobilize all existing resources; it can make
the whole economic and social system conform to the war
plan—including in the war plan the economic preparation for
war. It can distort the normal economy of the country and, if
the country is economically important enough, can distort the
economic life of its neighbours, can make the Jugoslavs take
aspirin in payment for raw materials, try to make the Americans take mouth-organs for cotton. It can accumulate stores
of raw materials, it can force on a rapid growth of substitutes,
replace natural materials with *Ersatz*, till the public almost
forgets the days when cloth was made of wool and coffee of
coffee. It can squeeze its neighbours till they find economic as
well as political reasons for wishing for an end of this nightmare; it can squeeze its own people until they almost wish for
war to end the strain of preparation. Fascinated by the problem of remaking the life of the community, increasingly
pleased with the virtuosity they have displayed, drunk with
power and, in modern Germany at any rate, corrupted by the
temptations that assail any controller of economic life who can
order when others have to bargain, the planners of the war
state lose sight of reality. The time comes when, like Roon in
1870, they dream of setting the whole machine in motion and
closing their desk, proud that everything has been foreseen.
At this stage they are bound to be far better prepared to fight
the war they have planned to fight than their victims who have
not planned to fight at all.

And now their disillusionment begins. Unless by a happy
accident (such as that which gave Roon the political genius of
Bismarck as cover) the political preparation has been perfectly
done, they have to fight a kindly war they did not plan to fight.
They have to fight a war that more and more states join in, for
the reason I have given, because they are too frightened not to.
Or the planners themselves get frightened, since their planned
superiority gets less as the other nations wake up and catch up
—and they make war as Hitler in 1941 invaded Russia—confident, oh so confident, that all will again go according to plan.

But it will not, for the plan is made in terms of military victory and that conception is not wide enough. There will have to be improvisations, changes, appeals to further total mobilizations and then further mobilizations. The initial technical advantages grow less every day; the material margin of superiority grows narrower every day, until the long victorious army finds victory, first sterile, then impossible.

But the history of the free state is very different. Of course, if that state is so limited in natural resources, or so vulnerable, that a predatory neighbour can overrun it in a few weeks, planning for war and total victory, whether done by Roon or by Goering, may seem to pay, as it seemed to pay in 1870 and 1940. *Seemed*, for the balance sheet of 1870 did not close with the Treaty of Frankfort, it was kept open for a generation later as Europe grew more and more militarized, more and more frightened of Gemany and Germany more and more frightened of Europe. 1918 is an item in that balance sheet; 1944 is an item in the balance sheet of 1940. But the free state that is not so overrun has many advantages when the first shock is overcome.

Its people do not expect miracles and do not have to be presented with a less and less plausible picture of infallible leaders whose impeccable plans somehow are not going right. A democratic state is resigned to less than total efficiency in its rulers, less than total success. Because it assumes some of the the responsibility for the decisions made, it assumes, too, part of the responsibility for the mistakes made. It can criticize its rulers—and itself—without losing its faith in either. It has not been, in fact, the leaders of the democracies who have been forced to invent or survive conspiracies, to find dramatic, diabolic excuses for failures, to repeat endless rhetorical appeals, to fall to the lowest demagoguery in face of bad news or collapse in infantile exultation at good. It has been Hitler who has behaved like an ill-bred brat in 1940 and has made hysterical appeals to Providence to save him and the Third Reich (in that order) in 1944.

But even on the material plane the free states gain in a long war. No battle, said Moltke, is ever fought as it is planned. Still less is any long war. The very adequacy of the pre-war plans is a handicap for the long war. The military state has already, with brilliant short-term results, taken over the economic and social life of the whole country. It has mobilized for war purposes all the national resources; it has decided how to invest the man-power, the material equipment, the basic wealth as well as the spiritual resources of the nation. But it is not creating any new resources. It is squeezing the orange but there is only one orange.

In the free state there are in existence a score of independent pools of power, material power, moral power. The individual citizen is now pouring into the national pool new resources he and his friends and partners have been creating all the time. Under the pressure of national danger he consents to be directed as to what to do with what he created in the time of peace. As the war winds on, never quite meeting the specifications of any plan, the free states are able to improvise, to adjust, to invent. There is butter to be turned into newer types of guns. There are talents, odd, original, insubordinate talents to be called on, there is an immense amount of wasteful, spontaneous life to be drawn on for war. It is not the naïve, peace-loving free states who find the rulers of their peoples looking, after a time, for magical remedies for the refusal of victory to come or, if it comes, to stay. It is not the democracies who fall for the witch-doctors or astrologers or for the panaceas, the invincible U-boat; the equally invincible Luftwaffe; the equally invincible and omnipotent secret weapon, No. 1, No. 2, etc. In the darkness that has been imposed for years on the people of the military state, it was easy to prepare for war; it was also easy to lose the habit of rational judgment, to acquire the appetite for miracles—and the habit of cursing the witch-doctors who have not wrought the miracles, cursing at first very secretly, then more openly.

One disability the peace-loving, anti-militarist nations *do* suffer from. In a country dominated by the army, like Prussia all though its history, like France under Napoleon, the army draws easily and naturally, in peace-time, on the most energetic and talented members of the nation. A very high proportion of the ablest young men will enter the army and make their careers in it. And, in consequence, planning for war in the technical sense will be more thoroughly, more competently carried out. The army in Britain, in America, even in a country like France, where it had lost a good deal of its old prestige, will not be so impressive an institution; its leaders may be, and will certainly be made to appear, mediocre and outmoded people. Again, the military state will win in the first stages of the war.

But just because war is now total this advantage will disappear as the war lasts. Even more important than the material reserves accumulated by the free action of the free citizen, or the moral resources bred by the habit of free choice, is the technical reserve bred by the civilian habit of life. For in the United States and Britain hundreds, thousands of men of great energy and initiative exist to be called into service in a great crisis. In the old days of limited warfare, when the main business was the application of a narrow technique, of drill, gunnery, tactics, the advantages of a very large class of trained officers were great. But in modern war they are much less. There is nothing specifically *military* about most of the problems of total war. The problem of planning for the invasion of France was ninety per cent non-military planning. The scores of types of landing craft needed were made and designed by the engineers of peace-time industry; it was Detroit and the Clyde that were called on; the varied, unplanned civilian resources of peaceful societies. The problems of designing a tank, or a war plane, or counter-measures against submarines, do not call for peace-time military organization, they call for technical skill and originality. And that technical skill and originality will be not less but more, because the peace-time organization has been looser, less organized, less directed to one end. The wind of discovery often bloweth where it listeth. More than that, peace technicians are always solving *real* problems, not merely planning to solve them. The difficulty that faces any military organization of making its problems real applies to its technical side too. Manœuvres are no substitute for war; the prototype no substitute for production for use. But peace-time industry produces for use; the jeep is the child of the flivver, the corvette of the freighter. Had Nazi preparations for war been spun out for another five years or so, had the Goering stranglehold on German industry lasted a few years longer, German industry would have been more effectually mobilized for immediate successes and even less well prepared for the long pull when the first successes did not prove to be enough. There would have been more magnetic mines, or their like; more reliance on improved submarines; more reliance on air-power. And there would have been even less material and intellectual preparation for the failure of these recipes for victory. The militarist state, facing a nation of the same or superior industrial capacity, will win the first round or the first laps. But any trainer of runners or boxers knows that it is the last lap and the last round that count. And he knows too that mere endless training in running and boxing is not enough; nor is running against the clock or shadow-boxing or boxing with sparring partners. The only way to train winners is to train them in many more things than running and boxing and more important still, the would-be winners must run real races frequently, fight real fights frequently. The champion who is not in the ring often ceases to be champion. Even the Prussian or Spartan state cannot be putting on real military contests all the time. But the civil society can be putting on innumerable real contests, civil contests, all the time; their technicians are always on their toes and the training they receive in peace is equally available in war. In a deeper sense than Milton probably meant it, "peace hath her victories no less renowned than war"—and that in war.

That the English and American nations escaped this professional distortion is not due to any special moral or intellectual virtue—at any rate, not exclusively due to it. England, as Michelet said, is an island. Much of English society owes its flavour to that fact, to the comparative immunity from immediate physical danger produced by that fact. America, for all practical purposes, is even more of an island. Both could afford to do without great standing armies. Both could afford to reduce to a minimum the intrusion of military methods into civil life. But it should be pointed out that being an island or being a remote group of settlements in an isolated continent is not, in itself, a guarantee against the follies of militarism. Japan is even more of an island than England—and Japan has turned the control of her life and polity over to militarist control as thoroughly as Prussia ever did. In some South American states, Paraguay in the past, Argentina in the present, the officers have been given a political predominance that they have never known in the United States. No, there is choice as well as fatality. And there is accident as well as choice. The accident was the happy fatality that gave the English-speaking peoples an ancestral distaste for the rule of soldiers and for the "leader principle." That fatality was the rule of Cromwell, so much misunderstood and foolishly exploited by the Nazis. For the rule of Cromwell and the New Model Army, vastly superior as were both to the rule of Hitler and his party army, yet left a legacy of great political value. An incurable dislike of military rule was bequeathed both to the English and American peoples—and a most hated name was bequeathed to the Irish.[1]

[1] A sign of the high degree of objectivity attained by the English ruling class at the height of its fame, when it alone had withstood Napoleon from the beginning to the end, is to be found in Henry Hallam's parallel between Cromwell and Napoleon. "In civil government there can be no adequate parallel between one who had sucked only the dregs of a besotted fanaticism, and one to whom the stores of reason and philosophy were open. But it must here be added that Cromwell, far unlike his antitype, never showed any signs of a legislative mind or any desire to fix his renown on that noblest human basis, the amelioration of social institutions." (Henry Hallam, *Constitutional History of England*.) What Hallam would have said if he had been asked to draw a parallel between Napoleon and his self-styled antitype, Hitler, is difficult to conceive. If Cromwell's naïve trust in the Old Testament was proof of besotted fanaticism, what would Hallam have said of the mind revealed in *Mein Kampf*? If Cromwell's failure to reform the English legal system was proof of limitations, what would he have said of the destruction of the idea of the rule of law, of even the concept of a *Rechtsstaat*, in the Third Reich? Many an Englishman and many an American was, in fact, awakened to the pathological character of the Third Reich by the literary tone of *Mein Kampf* (how right the Führer was to try to prevent publication of full translations!) and more by the destruction of any system of organized law in Germany. The dead spoke; the dead who had condemned the Cromwellian experiment to peaceful dissolution; the dead who had set up as the ideal of the American constitution-maker, "a government of laws and not of men."

Cromwell died in his bed. In less than two years the ever-victorious, highly disciplined army that seemed to have the English state and people at its mercy, dissolved. The old monarchy was restored, resting on law and custom, not on force. The 50,000 men of the New Model became a mere 5,000 or so, commanded by General Monk, who had no fanaticism, who had fought on both sides, and who, inspired as Professor Clark suggests by his experience in the service of the Dutch Republic, commended to his officers the example of the Dutch service "where soldiers received and observed commands, but gave none."

Even more striking is the way in which the American soldier, however highly esteemed and flattered, has been kept in firm submission to the civil power and has accepted, without question, that authority. It is no geographical phenomenon, as the case of the Latin-American states shows.

Mr. H. G. Wells is probably right in saying that Plutarch kept the United States a republic—and Plutarch, like all cultivated men of the ancient world, regretted the eclipse of the republican ideal. But Cromwell also helped; so did the memory of James II, who had feebly tried to rule by an army. It was after that experience that the English Parliament passed the Mutiny Act for one year at a time only; the mere existence of the army was at the annual mercy of Parliament and, then, when the American Constitution was created, at the mercy of Congress. Both Parliament and Congress sometimes carried their fear of militarism to absurd lengths; they starved the army in peace and harassed it in war. But they had their reward. They got great soldiers who were content to be great soldiers. Even so vehement a victorious general as Andrew Jackson submitted to the humiliating sentence of the civil court in that city of New Orleans which he had just saved by a brilliant victory. General Jackson obeyed as, later, President Jackson commanded. The Duke of Wellington had his windows broken fifteen years after Waterloo by a London mob that did not like his reactionary politics. He did not like it; he thought it was a little ungrateful; but, after all, he had entered politics and had to take the rough with the smooth.

In the American Civil War the federal government began with an army of 16,000 and ended it with an army of 2,000,000. At no time in the four years of brilliant improvisation had the awkward, ungainly civilian, Lincoln, the slightest reason to fear any of the military complications and threats of political action by generals that other less well ordered societies have known. His opposite number, Jefferson Davis, had the disadvantage of having had a professional military training and of having served in a real war. But despite the more and more obvious fact that he was temperamentally unfitted for his post, in face of increasing disaster, despite the overwhelming prestige of the great Southern general, Lee, the authority of the civil power remained uncontested to the bitter end. And, as defeat was inevitable anyway, the Southern soldiers and civilians who displayed these political virtues had their reward, not only in duty done but in a saving principle observed and saved to future use.

British and American generals have not been all models of disinterestedness or of single-minded devotion to the cause. They have been recruited, necessarily, from human beings. But an examination of their record does not show that they have been inferior in these qualities to the generals produced by societies which made the producing of generals their main business. It was in the German Army, in the last war, that General Max Hoffman was forced to say that if any more officers came to him promising their Nibelung-true support, he would knock their blocks off. It is in the German Army in this war that military conspiracy has reached up to Supreme Headquarters; it matters little who was conspiring against whom, or whether the motives of the conspirators were good or bad. The fact of conspiracy was decisive condemnation of a system of war-making that exalted blind obedience to heights which destroy both mind and character.

II

. One of the great blessings conferred on the professional
soldier by the firm control of the civil authority and by the
moral tone of the civil society he lives in, is freedom from a
professional code of honour and code of morals. Nothing is
more unintelligible to the English or American soldier than
the German conception of a special type of military honour.
An English or American officer is content to observe the
general code of a good citizen and an educated gentleman. He
has, as an officer, special duties, special obligations. But these
do not cut him off from his civilian friends or impose on him
standards of conduct unintelligible to civilians and hostile to
their standards. The officer does represent in a business society
a standard different from that of the mere profit-seeker, but
so does the doctor, the lawyer, the teacher, the preacher, or
priest. The army and navy have their special codes, but they
are inside the general code. There is no obligation on the
officer to fight duels in defence of his honour. That barbaric
custom died out in the army and civil life alike. There is no
obligation to kick civilians out of the way in defence of army
honour as was done in Saverne in 1914 or to run civilians
through for not getting out of the way quick enough. Neither
the British nor American armies have found it necessary to set
up courts of honour to create a pathological case law for a
caste. They have found adequate supplies of honour all the
same in many sources—including humour. It is in the German
Army, not the British or American Armies as we must recall,
that it was found necessary to set up a Court of Honour to try
generals for treason in war-time. Again it matters little whether
the really guilty men were the judges or judged. The basic
guilt was that of the system. If the military systems of America
and England only lost wars, their more reasonable, flexible,
less humourless view of the role of the officer might be condemned. But they win wars as well as making peace less barbaric. So did the Roman Republic in its great days when it

would allow no soldiers inside the sacred city and insisted on the pre-eminence of the civil power.

The soldier who is the servant of the free state suffers under many handicaps as a technician. He has to submit to the orders of amateurs who may have only a very imperfect understanding of his technical difficulties. He has to spend much time persuading civilians instead of giving orders; he is never sole master of his army, sole judge of what is to be done, when and how. It is easy to illustrate the dangers and delays such a relation causes. There is Marlborough having to argue with timid and ill-equipped Dutch deputies; there is McClellan alienating ill-informed American politicians in the Civil War because he failed in the art of persuasion; there is the friction between Clemenceau and Foch; there is the long story of Wellington dealing with Spaniards, with Portuguese, with the government at home, learning diplomacy and patience in the process. Patience—that, above all, the general of a free state learns; the sudden glory of lightning victory is not for him. He has to submit the mere art of arms to the greater art of politics. It is only when we look at the results, over a long period, that we begin to perceive that, even when war was a simpler, more limited thing than it can be to-day, the soldier did not really suffer from these limitations. He gained; he was trained in the general art of war (which is greater than the art of fighting) and, if he did not learn, he was saved from the worst mistakes. It is the pure technician who sacrifices everything to the battle who, in the long run, loses. The most brilliant soldier of the ancient world, Hannibal, was not ill served by the Carthaginian politicians. They provided him with all the resources they could command. The basic error was not that of the maligned Suffetes but of the brilliant soldier. It was his decision to attack Rome at the very heart of her power, in Italy, that was the basic error, the error that made Cannae a sterile technical triumph. For it was based on a false *political* calculation, that military victory would dissolve the Latin confederacy on whose unity depended the power and safety of Rome. Hannibal at the gates of Rome, Napoleon on the Channel in 1805, Hitler in Paris and on the Channel in 1940, learned that victory,

E

decisive victory, is a more elusive thing than mere triumph in the field and that mere concentration of political and military power in one politically incompetent hand is no recipe for victory, even though from a strictly military point of view all the elements of victory seem to be there.[1]

The military servant of a free state may gain more than he loses by his limited powers; he is saved from temptation as well as denied opportunities. But even if, on balance, he loses, the state does not. For it does not exist to exploit military virtuosity or to provide opportunities for its exercise by its generals. In a free state war and victory must have desirable peace-time results. Even so war-making a people as the Romans knew that.

"Hae tibi erunt artes *pacisque imponere morem.*" To impose the habit of peace was the aim of Roman war. When that aim was forgotten, when the military servants of the Republic became its masters, the life of the republic was doomed; the Consul sank into the mere Imperator, the Feldherr, the Führer. *Nostra stultitia tu es magnus* as the Roman wit said of the greatness of Pompey, the victorious general, the head of a party. By the political folly of the Roman people, he became great to give way, in time, to Caesar. And it was not Caesar, the Imperator *par excellence*, but that much more sedate and civilian figure, Augustus, who for two or three generations, postponed the crisis of the Roman state but could not for ever avoid the consequences of the passing of all effective political power to the army.

[1] The judgment of the Duke of Wellington on his great rival is worth noting in its probably unconscious revelation of the truth. "Lady Salisbury asked which was the greatest military genius, Marlborough or Napoleon? 'Why, I don't know—it is very difficult to tell. I can hardly conceive anything greater than Napoleon at the head of any army—especially a French army. Then he had one prodigious advantage—he had no responsibility— he could do whatever he pleased; and *no man ever lost more armies than he did*. Now with me the loss of every man told. I could not risk so much; I knew that if I ever lost five hundred men without the clearest necessity, I should be brought upon my knees to the bar of the House of Commons." (Stanhope, *Conversations with Wellington.*) (Italics mine.) Wellington, like Washington, was saved from the temptations of military omnipotence. He was also saved from the risk of a Jena or a Waterloo *lost.*

From a great event in modern history the Germans might learn the same lesson. For it is taught them by a German leader and by the people of a state that they profess to regard as Germanic. William the Silent of Nassau was faced, as leader of the revolted Netherlands, with an almost insoluble military problem. How was he, a mediocre general with a badly organized state in the process of formation, to resist great generals like Alva and Parma at the head of technically perfect Spanish armies? All his plans were handicapped, were limited by the power of the Dutch towns and provinces; no war leader had less of a free hand or had to spend more of his time in mere persuasion, mere politics. With more unquestioned power William might have scored more military successes, might have negotiated with more confidence and decision, would have had to possess his soul far less often in patience. But not only might he, like Napoleon, have lost it in the process, the result of the war would have been very different. Victory might have come sooner but it would have been a very different and less permanent victory. Indeed, the war would not have been fought at all. If the Dutch cities and provinces on the fringe of the "Holy Roman Empire of the German People" had not been obstinate, individualistic, political, they would not have rebelled. If they had not had the good fortune to have been educated by the Burgundian dynasty into a sense of the general interest of the state without being coerced into mere automatic submission to the will of the prince, they would not have dared to face the armies of Philip II of Spain.

And if, in the course of the war, they *had* put all their trust in any one prince, had abandoned their political attitude, their victory would have been far less interesting to the world; it would have been a mere Prussian victory. But it was the free Dutch Republic that produced in the next generations Rembrandt and Grotius, Vermeer and Huygens, that provided cities of refuge for Descartes and Spinoza. That Dutch Republic was, and is, of permanent interest to the whole world; there is no German state in the seventeenth century whose history and achievement concerns anybody but Germans—and not many of them have a history that concerns even Germans. In 1940 the Dutch summoned to return to their Germanic Fatherland were secured against any temptation to do so by the memory of their great, free, proud past. No more than in 1580 were they prepared to accept the German view of the decisiveness of mere victory and mere power. It was not the Dutch Protestants or, indeed, the Dutch Catholics who had accepted the German rule that the religion of the ruler was to determine the religion of his subjects. And they had their reward in sources of dignified, not hysterical and illusion-fed national pride. Of course the Dutch were luckier than the Germans of the seventeenth century. To that luck they owe their rich culture, their rich national life, their rich empire. How could any of these, even the empire, have been built by docile obedience to the rulers as by God appointed? But the *character* of Dutch luck is ignored by the merely envious German. The real Dutch luck was the historical accident that forced them to accept responsibility, that forced them to take sides, not merely to obey the local authority, however silly, however petty. The party conflicts that harassed William the Silent, that led to the death of Oldenbarnveldt and John de Witt, to the long feud between the burgher aristocracy and the House of Orange, this was the luck of the Dutch. The German subjects of the elder line of Nassau were saved from party war; the burgher aristocracy of Emden or Frankfort were saved from the dangers and temptations of real political power and responsibility. And with them were saved great philosophers like Leibniz, great architects like Fischer, saved to be, in various ways, courtiers of genius. The Dutch refused, in the seventeenth and twentieth centuries alike, the conception of leadership as Germans have accepted it; the orders given from above, obeyed uncritically, loyally, bravely from below. The people that resisted Philip II and Louis XIV were not likely to accept the authority of Hitler or see political and national promotion in acceptance as second-class members of a Germanic race whose highest political expression was fanatical obedience to such a chief.

The nineteenth century illustrated the difference between the political and the military victory in a way that suggests the work of a great dramatist. Lincoln and Bismarck, the raw, self-educated, humorous American, the highly educated, cynical, witty Prussian. Both were sceptical, but Bismarck was sceptical of the good faith, the honesty, the good sense of the masses; Lincoln was sceptical of there being any greater dose of these good qualities in the rulers. He was also sceptical of himself. Bismarck had had his republican, his Jacobin past, but he had chosen another and more profitable way. And these men, at the same time, were making or saving the union of their peoples. The unity of the German people was made, as Bismarck boasted, not by speeches or by slogans but by "blood and iron." The American union was saved by far more blood and far more iron than was needed to unite Germany. But Lincoln, as resolute in making war as Bismarck, did not for a moment believe that all that was needed was blood and iron. He thought speeches were needed; that is why he stated the classical doctrine of American democracy on the victorious battlefield of Gettysburg. Bismarck had nothing to say at Sedan. That is why with victory in sight Lincoln pleaded, in the Second Inaugural, for a just peace and admitted the share of all Americans in the national sin of slavery. These speeches, as much as the Union preserved in arms, are the legacy of Lincoln. The legacy of Bismarck was an evasion of the political problem of how to make the German people politically mature; the legacy of Bismarck was a political system that left fatal decisions to a dilettante like William II, to a mere military technician like Ludendorff and then to that obscene parody of Lincoln, that product of the political childishness of the German people, Hitler, the demagogue without style and without truth. Compare the permanence of Lincoln's victory with the constant strain that was imposed on even the material achievement of Bismarck. If Bismarckian unity survives at all, it will survive in a mutilated form—and it will have had to be paid for in two great lost wars, more expensive in blood and iron than the American Civil War in which the mere efficiency experts could find so much to learn—if they were capable of learning.

But Germany is in Europe, not in America; Germany has

jealous neighbours. "We can't be carp because the others are pike," said Bismarck. There is truth in that. But think how much Germany has suffered by her mere military victories, by the absence of any power of *attraction* in the militarized German culture. Even when Napoleonic militarism had driven the peoples as well as the governments of Europe to detest many things called French, French culture, as Goethe said, was too much the inheritance of every civilized European for the invading armies not to be awestruck at the idea of occupying Paris. For many Europeans, Weimar and Salzburg and Vienna and Frankfort have some, though not of course anything like as much appeal as Paris or Rome or Florence. But for whom has Berlin any appeal except Berliners? For whom has modern German culture, with its self-willed return to barbarism, with its exaltation of the irrational, with its worship of force, with its disdain of argument and persuasion, any spontaneous attraction? Let the horror that filled the world in 1940 when it was thought for a moment possible that the future of Europe might be determined by the Third Reich be the answer. More striking still, let the answer be the anguish with which the desperate defence of England was watched. Where in Europe were the friends of the new Germany at the very moment of its highest material triumph? Where were the friends of the long unpopular English? Let the roll-call be made, the Quislings and Musserts and Lavals against the peoples of their betrayed countries, against the élite of the modern world. For London was one of the great makers and centres of modern civilization; great names fought on the English side; great English names, great German names. On which side stood the spirit of Leibniz or of Lessing, of Schiller or of Goethe? It was no accident that, in the dark hour, the opening bars of the Fifth Symphony were taken over by the resistance movement *against* the triumphant Germans. For could anyone doubt where was the spirit of Beethoven? It may be only a legend, but it is a suggestive legend, that makes Beethoven alter the dedication of the "Eroica" to the "memory of a great man" on receipt of the news that his hero Bonaparte has sunk into a mere Emperor. Could he have consented to the more than Byzantine flattery demanded by his fellow-Austrian? Could the Mozart of the *Magic Flute* have so surrendered? By their fruits shall ye know them. By its friends shall ye know the Third Reich; its friends in victory, its rats in defeat. But it is not only the Third Reich that has sacrificed so much to gain so little. It is the Prussian state, since the days of Frederick-William I. In discipline, in courage, in material honesty, in industry, the military and civil servants of the Prussian state have been, in many cases, models. But that state has not achieved the one thing necessary, a real political life in which these minor virtues can have their place. And so its victories have been sterile and its defeats its own private business, lamented by few. Far other has been the destiny of less organized, more hopeful, less "efficient" societies, of France, of England, of the United States, of the Netherlands.

Their friends in evil fortune,

> "... are exultations, agonies,
> And love, and man's unconquerable mind."